CRAVE
BOSTON

The Urban Girl's Manifesto

Melody Biringer

The Urban Girl's Manifesto

We CRAVE Community.
At CRAVE Boston we believe in acknowledging, celebrating, and passionately supporting local businesses. We know that, when encouraged to thrive, neighborhood establishments enhance communities and provide rich experiences not usually encountered in mass-market. By introducing you to the savvy businesswomen in this guide, we hope that CRAVE Boston will help inspire your own inner entrepreneur.

We CRAVE Adventure.
We could all use a getaway, and at CRAVE Boston we believe that you don't need to be a jet-setter to have a little adventure. There's so much to do and explore right in your own backyard. We encourage you to break your routine, to venture away from your regular haunts, to visit new businesses, to explore all the funky finds and surprising spots that Boston has to offer. Whether it's to hunt for a birthday gift, indulge in a spa treatment, order a bouquet of flowers, or connect with like-minded people, let CRAVE Boston be your guide for a one-of-a-kind hometown adventure.

We CRAVE Quality.
CRAVE Boston is all about quality products and thoughtful service. We know that a satisfying shopping trip requires more than a simple exchange of money for goods, and that a rejuvenating spa date entails more than a quick clip of the cuticles and a swipe of polish. We know you want to come away feeling uplifted, beautiful, excited, relaxed, relieved and, above all, knowing you got the most bang for your buck. We have scoured the city to find the hidden gems, new hot spots, and old standbys, all with one thing in common: they're the best of the best!

A Guide to Our Guide

CRAVE Boston is more than a guidebook. It's a savvy, quality-of-lifestyle book devoted entirely to the best local businesses owned by women. CRAVE Boston will direct you to more than 100 local spots—top boutiques, spas, cafés, stylists, fitness studios, and more. And we'll introduce you to the inspired, dedicated women behind these exceptional enterprises, for whom creativity, quality, innovation, and customer service are paramount. Not only is CRAVE Boston an intelligent guidebook for those wanting to know what's happening throughout town, it's a directory for those who value the contributions that spirited businesswomen make to our city.

Consumer Business Section
Consumer-driven entreprenesses, including boutiques, spas, and food.

Intelligentsia Section
Business-to-business entreprenesses, including coaching, marketing and public relations, photography, business consulting, and design services.

CRAVE Categories

Abode	Furniture, home improvement, and interior design
Adorn	Jewelry
Children's	Baby-, children-, and mom-related
Conncot	Networking, media, technology, travel, and event services
Details	Gifts, books, small home accessories, florists, and stationery
Enhance	Spas, salons, beauty, and fitness
Pets	Pet-related
Sip Savor	Food and drink
Style	Clothing, shoes, eyewear, handbags, and stylists

What is your indulgence?

" *Don't save your best china for a special day. Make every day special. Live life with zest.* "

Betsy Merry of MerryFoxRealty

5S PUBLIC RELATIONS

450 Harrison Ave, Ste 305, Boston, 617.426.1806
5spr.com, Twitter: @5spr

Committed. Aggressive. Effective.
Utilizing traditional media and social networking platforms, 5sPR consistently and aggressively achieves results, plain and simple. They ensure that your message is always delivered to the right audience, because they believe it's not about being loud ... it's about being heard.

Jessica deGuardiola

Q and A

What are your most popular products or services?
Securing media coverage. It's thrilling to
know we've taken under-the-radar companies
and turned them into household names.

What business mistake have you
made that you will not repeat?
Making decisions based on emotion.
I've learned the importance of taking
a step back and "sleeping on it."

Where is your favorite place to
go with your girlfriends?
Brunch. By the second Mimosa, the dirt's
been divulged, day-to-day crises analyzed,
and we're laughing so hard we're in tears.

What do you CRAVE? In business? In life?
A challenge. Some of my proudest moments in
business, and in life, for that matter, happened
when all the odds were against me.

Sharon Perkins-Allen

Q and A

What are your most popular products or services?
The most popular berry changes like the wind. However, we sell a lot of peanut butter berries and caramel berries. Most customers are surprised by these flavors.

What or who inspired you to start your business?
I grew up in an entrepreneurial household. My parents encouraged us to dream big and have faith. If that meant starting a chocolate-covered strawberry business, then so be it—they encouraged me to go for it!

What business mistake have you made that you will not repeat?
Because I do something I love, I didn't push the business in the beginning. If you want your business to be successful, you have to market it.

A CHOCOLATE DIP

800.678.9819
achocolatedip.com, Twitter: @achocolatedip

Passionate. Vivacious. Delectable.
Experience true love when you bite into one of A Chocolate Dip's juicy sweet strawberries, hand-picked and hand-dipped in your choice of decadent chocolate and scrumptious toppings. The utmost care is put into A Chocolate Dip's product, which will leave you yearning for more.

Photos by Renee Trichilo

A GIRL'S GOTTA GO

617.314.7266
agirlsgottago.com, Twitter: @agirlsgottago

High-flying. Accommodating. Rejuvenating.
A Girl's Gotta Go specializes in vacation packages for women and those they travel with. When you're busy juggling a family, a successful career, and a packed social calendar, it's important to take some time out and get away from it all. A Girl's Gotta Go will get you there for your amazing vacation!

Photos by Leigh Smyth of Oh Snap! photography

COPLEY PLAZ
A FAIRMONT HOTE
1912

Stacy Evos

 Q and A

What are your most popular products or services?
Some popular destinations are Italy, Bermuda,
the Greek Islands, and Barbados. Cruising
and spa vacations are also very popular.

People may be surprised to know...
A portion of our proceeds benefit breast
cancer research, education, screening, and
treatment. Now, that's worth traveling for!

How do you spend your free time?
I love to cook, shop, and travel, and enjoy
these activities most with family and friends.

Where is your favorite place to
go with your girlfriends?
Nantucket. We go every summer, and
I look forward to it each year.

What is your indulgence?
Good food, good wine, and, of course, travel!

What are your most popular products or services?
My fall conference, SHINE: Discover Your True Wealth™, draws 1,000 women entrepreneurs from all over the globe.

People may be surprised to know...
When I first started my business, there was a point when I had less than $20 to my name.

Who is your role model or mentor?
Entrepreneurs such as Oprah Winfrey, Mary Kay Ash, and Richard Branson inspire me.

What business mistake have you made that you will not repeat?
At first, I thought I had to figure it all out alone. Today, I have mentors and a team to support me.

Ali Brown

live your good fortune®

ali flip

Main photo (this page) and portrait by Lesley Bohm, bottom right photo (opposite page) by Greg Crowder

ALI MAGAZINE

888.484.5559
thealimagazine.com, Twitter: @alibrownla

Fun. Dynamic. Brazen.
Ali Magazine is business, life, and style for the entrepreneurial woman—all wrapped up in a gorgeous, full-color, quarterly publication. From phenomenal female moguls to dressing for success, there's nothing else like it.

Amye Kurson

Q and A

What or who inspired you to
start your business?
I was inspired to start Ame & Lulu as a
new golfer who wanted appealing, feminine
headcovers for my clubs. I could not find this
product, and discovered there was a much-
needed market for women's golf accessories.

How do you spend your free time?
I love to shop around, especially at antique
shops and flea markets, to find props for photo
shoots and new design ideas. I am constantly
inspired by colors and patterns and always
thinking about what we can come up with next.

What do you CRAVE? In business? In life?
Ame & Lulu being a successful lifestyle
brand while I find balance between
my family and personal life.

AME & LULU

617.730.9604
ameandlulu.com

Stylish. Vibrant. Practical.
Ame & Lulu is a sophisticated lifestyle brand that embraces classic American
style. Products include golf, tennis, yoga, and everyday accessories. The signature
product line, Golf, caters to many golf pro shops and resorts who use the products as
tournament tee prizes. The pet, baby, and home collections were launched in 2010.

Erica Farthing

 *Q and A*

What or who inspired you to start your business?
As a real estate broker, I was always trying to make real estate interesting and fun. When I began to host events in otherwise vacant spaces, a vibrant sense of new life was created.

What do you CRAVE? In business? In life?
What I crave changes constantly. I'm always seeking my next challenge in life. I want to look back 30 years from now and realize that the company I started at 25 was only the beginning.

Where is your favorite place to go with your girlfriends?
Brunch is my all-time favorite activity. There's nothing better than catching up with your girls over mimosas, preferably with lots of sunshine.

ASSEMBLY

319 A St, Boston, 617.849.4993
assemblyboston.com, Twitter: @assemblyboston

Lively. Urban. Chic.
Assembly is a full-service event location, production, and management company for social, corporate, and non-profit events. Their solid understanding of the real-estate market enables them to find interesting event venues. Whether it's a brick-and-beam style loft or sleek penthouse, Assembly caters to all aspects of event planning and design with their artistic vision and selection of vendors.

Photos by Melissa Ostrow

17

ATHALIA ORIGINALS

617.512.6228
athaliaoriginals.com

Unique. Creative. Stylish.
Athalia Originals produces one-of-a-kind, handmade jewelry in sterling silver
and semi-precious stones. See Athalia's designs at arts-and-crafts shows
throughout New England, at boutiques, or schedule your own home party with
all your friends! There is something for everyone who loves jewelry.

Photos by Leigh Smyth of Oh Snap! photography

Emily Athalia Hirsch

Q and A

What are your most popular products or services?
My signature piece, the flowered choker.

People may be surprised to know...
I am a self-taught jewelry designer,
and no piece is ever duplicated.

What or who inspired you to start your business?
Wanting to be creative in a mass-produced
world. There is no better feeling than seeing
something I designed being worn by one
of my fantastic and loyal customers.

Where is your favorite place to
go with your girlfriends?
Our neighborhood restaurant, Harry's.

What do you CRAVE? In business? In life?
Success and happiness in my career
and with my creations. I want women to
enjoy my designs as much as I do!

B'AIRES

81 Wareham St, Boston, 866.399.6393
bairesusa.com, Twitter: @welcometobaires

Avant-garde. Worldly. Modern.
B'aires is an agent and showroom for high-end South American designers. The showroom features distinctive fashion-forward luxury goods—from sculpted, handmade jewelry lines to edgy, urban-inspired Buenos Aires street wear to luxurious shawls and wraps. Working directly with the designers as an agent, b'aires sells their products to award-winning boutiques around the country.

Sarah Pemberton

Q and A

What are your most popular products or services?
Gabriela Horvat sterling hammered bangles
do very well for us. We are excited about
a new line designed specifically for b'aires
by an Art Basel sculptress, Silvia Gai.

People may be surprised to know...
Hot dogs are my favorite food. Seriously.

What or who inspired you to start your business?
Junior year abroad in Australia. The markets
in Sydney housed really cool designers
that were underexposed and got me
thinking about the global fashion trade.

Who is your role model or mentor?
Mark Cuban. I love people who don't
apologize for who they are.

How do you spend your free time?
Reading, running, cooking, going to
the beach, traveling, and dancing.

Sheri Falk

Q and A

What are your most popular
products or services?
Wardrobe consultation.

People may be surprised to know...
We wear 20 percent of our clothes
80 percent of the time.

What or who inspired you to
start your business?
Fashion should not be so hard!

Who is your role model or mentor?
Donna Karan.

What business mistake have you
made that you will not repeat?
Not listening to my own instincts.

How do you spend your free time?
With my 2-year-old daughter, Gigi.

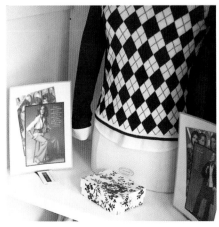

BASIQUES

172 Newbury St, Boston, 857.445.0144
basiques.com, Twitter: @basiques1

Simple. Classic. Elegant.
One complete wardrobe. One suitcase. BASIQUES offers style that is classic
and feminine. Stop by BASIQUES and learn how to pack just a few pieces and
maximize combinations, how to fit and flatter your frame, how to be feminine
without being flirty, and, most importantly, how to look good and feel great!

What or who inspired you
to start your business?

"*That first box of
64 Crayolas.*"

Jane Brunelle of Eye 4 Color

Carson M. Eddy

 Q and A

What or who inspired you to
start your business?
A lifelong passion for personal adornment
inspired me to cultivate a business that
would inspire, teach, and encourage women
of all ages to wear beautiful jewelry they
had designed and made themselves.

People may be surprised to know...
I earned my MFA in costume design from
Carnegie-Mellon University, and I taught
at Tufts University for nearly 20 years
before becoming a business owner.

How do you spend your free time?
I spend my free time eating home-cooked
meals with my husband, and talking to our
grown son about his career as an artist and
our daughter about her career in fashion.

BEADWORKSHOP

23 Church St, Cambridge, 617.868.9777
10 Front St, Salem, 978.741.2323
beadworkshops.com

Colorful. Ever-changing. Creative.
BEADworkshop boutiques are overflowing with an ever-changing selection of the finest
beads, gemstones, pearls, seed beads, findings, tools, books, ready-made jewelry, and
accessories. Owner Carson M. Eddy travels extensively to acquire the beads, gemstones,
and findings for her retail stores. In addition to offering a glorious selection of beads,
they have an extensive schedule of classes, in-store parties, and repair services.

Photos by Renee Trucillo, except portrait by L. Stacy Eddy

27

BELLA BRIDESMAID

85 Newbury St, 2nd Floor, Boston, 617.755.6273
bellabridesmaid.com

Fresh. Sassy. Chic.
Bella Bridesmaid is a quaint and inviting boutique that offers a refreshing departure
from the usual bridesmaid experience: fresh, sassy, and chic designer dresses
in an intimate, upscale, and approachable setting. Realizing the important role
of a bridesmaid dress, Bella Bridesmaid provides each bride with personalized
attention in a one-on-one environment filled with the latest designer dresses.

Photos by Leigh Smyth of Oh Snap! photography

Brittan McCarthy

What or who inspired you to start your business?
I've been a bridesmaid more times than one can imagine, and I know the challenges my friends have faced to find their dresses. I knew Bella was a perfect fit for Boston and New England brides!

What business mistake have you made that you will not repeat?
Cutting corners. There is a lot of work that goes on behind the scenes with the ordering process, and sometimes you want to rush through It. I've learned it is so important to follow our process for every single order to ensure no detail is overlooked.

What do you CRAVE? In business? In life?
I crave the unexpected! I love the simple surprises that can pop up on any given day, whether at work or in my personal life, that put a smile on my face!

BLUSH HAIR SALON

1241 Massachusetts Ave, Arlington, 781.483.3500
blushhair.com, Twitter: @blushhair

Modern. Relaxed. Sophisticated.
Blush Hair Salon is dedicated to the evolution of hairstyling and the art of the craft.
Their ongoing education provides clients with a broad spectrum of styling options
tailored to their individual needs, while keeping up with the latest trends. Their goal is
for clients to leave the salon with the ability to recreate their new look day after day.

Photos by Janel Robertson

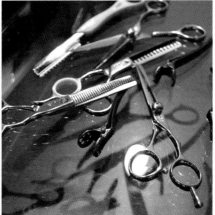

Kate Corcoran

 **Q** and **A**

People may be surprised to know...
Blush has three New York-trained color and
cutting specialists in Arlington Heights.

What or who inspired you to start your business?
My desire to provide style in a casual,
comfortable, and less pretentious environment.

Who is your role model or mentor?
I had many great stylists and teachers
that I learned from, but I was most
influenced by my business partner to
provide high-value services to clients.

How do you spend your free time?
With my husband and dog, cooking.

What is your indulgence?
Massages and really great food.

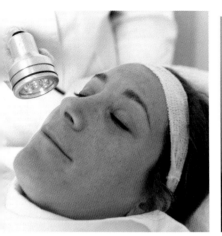

Bridget M. Riley

Q and A

What are your most popular
products or services?
Always hair removal! The HydraFacial
and Dermaroller are catching up, though.
The most popular product is definitely
Hylunia Facial Day Lotion, SPF 15.

People may be surprised to know...
Laser hair removal doesn't always work. But
that's okay, because electrolysis works for
everyone. It's precise, gentle, and guaranteed.
And we really do the best treatments in Boston.

What or who inspired you to
start your business?
All of my friends, family, and patients who kept
telling me to do it. At some point, you realize
that they are pushing you for a reason.

How do you spend your free time?
Reading anything I can get my hands on.

BOSTON SKIN SOLUTIONS

1318 Beacon St, Ste 7, Brookline, 617.334.4166
bostonskinsolutions.com

Innovative. Regenerative. Transformative.
Boston Skin Solutions is the city's premier destination for personal image enhancement, offering expert electrolysis, laser hair removal, and skin treatments. All treatments and products are physician formulated and certified organic. Boston Skin Solutions is proud to be the only office in the Boston area certified to perform genuine Dermaroller treatments.

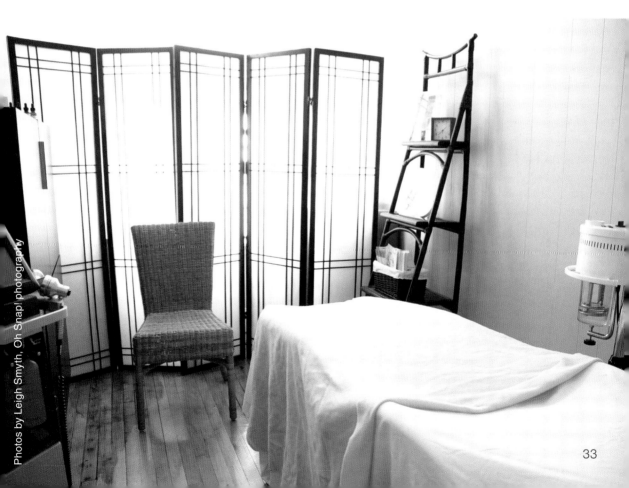

Photos by Leigh Smyth, Oh Snap! photography

BOW STREET FLOWERS

108 Beacon St, Somerville, 617.492.0080
bowstreetflowers.com, Twitter: @bowstreettweets

Old world. Fanciful. Unique.
From its beginnings in Harvard Square, Bow Street Flowers has always adhered to its passionate devotion to outstanding customer service and beautiful flowers. Its rustic interior is a perfect complement to elegant orchids, garden roses, and seasonal flowers displayed on antique tables and shelves. They maintain Old World artisan standards of floral design, creating arrangements and bouquets unique to each and every customer.

Shelley White

People may be surprised to know...
We have four rabbits who live in our shop.

What or who inspired you to start your business?
Maaderlake, a New York shop that is now closed.

Who is your role model or mentor?
I have flower crushes. Right now it's Kate Holt
of Flowerwild in Los Angeles. Recently, it was
Lewis Miller of LMD Floral in New York.

What business mistake have you
made that you will not repeat?
Not having a good bookkeeper.

What is your indulgence?
The iPad.

Where is your favorite place to
go with your girlfriends?
Snug Harbor Farm in Kennebunkport, Maine.

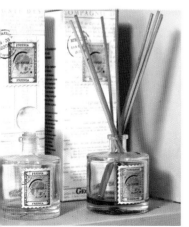

Cibeline
Sariano

Q and A

What are your most popular products or services?
Locally made designer clothing, must-have handbags, and exquisite jewelry.

People may be surprised to know...
The garments are designed by me, the fabric is sourced in the United States, and it's all produced in Massachusetts.

What or who inspired you to start your business?
Walking Madison Avenue at age 7.

What business mistake have you made that you will not repeat?
Over-purchasing.

Where is your favorite place to go with your girlfriends?
Toro for margaritas and tapas.

CIBELINE BOSTON

120 Charles St, Boston, 617.742.0244
cibelinesariano.com

Vibrant. Sophisticated. Approachable.
Cibeline Boston is the namesake boutique of fashion designer Cibeline Sariano, who designs clothes for real women of all shapes and personally helps them build distinguished wardrobes. Her collection is classic and tailored with a feminine twist, using a lush array of color. Visit this boutique and leave looking beautiful and feeling vibrant from head to toe.

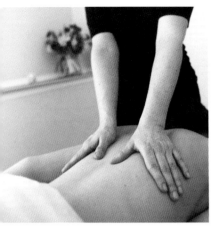

Ellen Comerford

Q and A

People may be surprised to know...
We're not just a warm, inviting boutique! Peek inside to see an inspiring Gyrotonic® and Pilates studio, a sunny group fitness room, and a tranquil spa nestled downstairs!

What or who inspired you to start your business?
I wanted to create a community where everyone—clients and employees—felt their best. My mission is to create a space that inspires the community to revel in a healthy, vibrant body, and to embrace wellness—body, mind, soul, and lifestyle.

What business mistake have you made that you will not repeat?
Making decisions from my head instead of my heart.

CORE DE VIE

40 Charles St, Boston, 617.720.0411
The Pilot House, Lewis Wharf, Boston, 617.720.0411
coredevie.com, Twitter: @CoredeVie

Holistic. Transformative. Nurturing.
Core de Vie is Boston's most unique spa and wellness center, offering best-in-class treatments including massages, facials, acupuncture, and craniosacral therapy. The movement center offers individual and semiprivate instruction in yoga, Pilates, Gyrotonic®, and Yamuna body rolling, as well as nutrition and health coaching. The boutique features high-quality activewear and wellness products, such as lululemon athletica, Vibram Five Fingers, and more!

Photos by Melissa Ostrow

COVEN

281 Essex St, Salem, 978.741.0500
Twitter: @covensalem

Artisanal. Fun. Delicious.
Coven is an artisanal market, café, and dessert bar featuring scratch-baked
cupcakes and other desserts, coffee, produce, cheeses, sandwiches, prepared
foods, and more. Coven provides unique, natural, and gourmet food in a fun setting.
They even have a cereal and cupcake bar, and lots of nostalgic decor.

Photos by Renee Trichilo

Jennifer Vourlos

Q and A

What are your most popular products or services?
Cupcakes, salted caramel brownies,
and the cereal bar!

People may be surprised to know...
We have retro Saturday morning cartoons
playing much of the day.

What or who inspired you to start your business?
My passion for feeding people yummy food
made from scratch with quality ingredients.

Who is your role model or mentor?
My mom, Jeanna, and my boyfriend's mom, Linda.
Two very strong women who teach me all the time.

How do you spend your free time?
Relaxing! If it is nice out, walking around
town and enjoying life slowly.

CRAVE26 EVENTS

774.287.5609
crave26events.com, Twitter: @Crave26Events

Stylish. Sophisticated. Inventive.
Crave26 Events is a full-service event-planning company serving the entire United States.
Crave26 Events specializes in, but is not limited to, social, destination, media, public relations, promotional, and high-profile events, as well as fashion shows, entertainment, and launch parties.

Meredith R. Bond

Q and A

What are your most popular products or services?
Full event-planning services. However, people really like to use individual services, such as on-site coordination or budget planning.

People may be surprised to know...
Aside from event planning, we also offer event coaching. This is for people who have all the tools but need a little guidance.

What or who inspired you to start your business?
My parents, Louis G. Bond and Robert Layne, inspired me to start my business. They are exceptional entrepreneurs and businessmen themselves. I would be a fool not to take something from them and follow in their footsteps.

What is your indulgence?
My biggest indulgence has to be shopping. Yes, I know it's typical, but I definitely get a feeling of euphoria when I find that great buy.

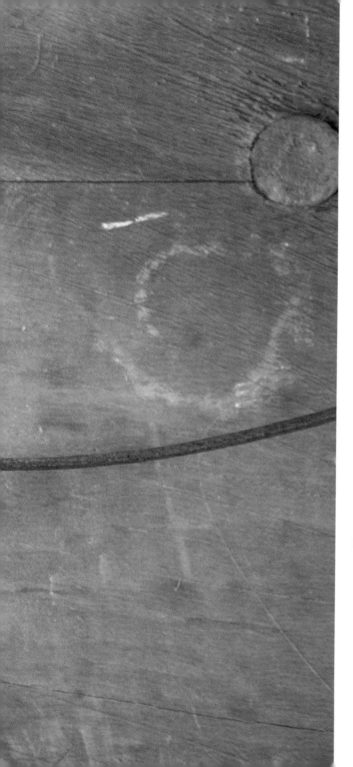

What business mistake
have you made that
you will not repeat?

*"Straying from our
ideals in an attempt
to please everyone.
We have found our
greatest success
in remaining true
to our original
concept."*

Deb Colburn of NOMAD

CRUSH BOUTIQUE

131 Charles St, Boston, 617.720.0010
shopcrushboutique.com, Twitter: @crushboutique

Coquettish. Congenial. Chic.
Crush Boutique offers the style-savvy woman a personal shopping experience
that can't be matched. The warm, cozy atmosphere and attentive staff will make
you feel at home as you revitalize your wardrobe with an eclectic mix of clothing,
shoes, and accessories by New York- and Los Angeles-based designers.

Photos by Leigh Smyth of Oh Snap! photography

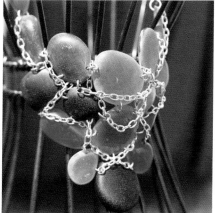

Rebecca Penner
and Laura Macris

Q and A

What are your most popular products or services?
Customers come to Crush for the overall
experience. We personally style you with
clothing and accessories from an eclectic mix
of designers. Customers particularly love our
darling cocktail frocks, well-priced accessories,
and fun, flirty tops for work or play.

Where is your favorite place to
go with your girlfriends?
One of our favorite places to unwind is the
Beehive, where you can enjoy live music
while indulging in amazing food and drinks.

What do you CRAVE? In business? In life?
Variety. In everything we do, we seek variety—
from the designers and looks we carry at
Crush, to the merchandising in the store, to
the places we travel, to the music we listen
to. It keeps things fresh and exciting!

DAVIS SQUARED

409 Highland Ave, Somerville, 617.666.6700
davissquared.com

Urban. Vibrant. Unique.
Go to Davis Squared for that special gift. Situated in the heart of Davis Square, they
are grateful to be part of such an amazing local scene. All of the beautiful items
are chosen with care, making the overall shopping experience truly unique.

Melisa Ford Christie

Q and A

What are your most popular products or services?
We have an incredible selection of thoughtful and thought-provoking greeting cards.

People may be surprised to know...
I received a bachelor of fine arts in acting from Emerson College.

What or who inspired you to start your business?
My husband. He has always been my biggest fan.

Who is your role model or mentor?
My best friends, Frank Zontini and Ken Tilton.

What is your indulgence?
Fancy cocktails with my gal pals!

Where is your favorite place to go with your girlfriends?
My favorite local restaurant, Gargoyles on the Square.

Melissa Babb

 Q and A

What are your most popular
products or services?
The DIY Package. It's for those who
want to do it themselves but need
help with the arts and crafts.

What or who inspired you to
start your business?
Lisa Hoffman, a wonderful invitation
designer and entrepreneur in New York.

Who is your role model or mentor?
My hospitality management professor
in college, Claudia Green. She works
incredibly hard for everything that she has.

Where is your favorite place to
go with your girlfriends?
At one of our apartments, cooking dinner
and watching romantic movies.

ENDLESS ELEGANZA EVENTS

978.618.4582
endlesseleganza.com, Twitter: @endlesseleganza

Fun. Friendly. Fabulous.
Endless Eleganza Events takes away the stress and leaves you the fun! Through creative design and careful attention to detail, they create thoughtful events that everyone will enjoy.

Photos by One Love Photography, except portrait by Renee Trichilo

EYE 4 COLOR

508.932.2820

Expressive. Encompassing. Energetic.
Eye 4 Color provides expert color scheme solutions for your home. Owner Jane Brunelle's fine art and interior design background, blended with 15 years of experience and extensive knowledge of color theory, is not something you can receive from a paint chip. She custom mixes colors, creating a unique palette designed specifically for your surroundings. The possibilities are limitless!

Photos by Nina Gallant

Jane Brunelle

 Q and A

What are your most popular products or services?
Color design, consultation, interior
design, and redesign.

People may be surprised to know...
There is no such thing as an ugly color.

Who is your role model or mentor?
Donald Kaufman, an incredible color theorist.

How do you spend your free time?
Enjoying my children, reading, cooking,
having fun with friends, and skiing.

What is your indulgence?
Starting a novel and not putting
it down until I finish it.

Where is your favorite place to
go with your girlfriends?
One of their kitchens for a great meal and laughter.

Jacqueline Albanese

Q and A

What are your most popular products or services?
Fresh flower arrangements for weddings and events.

What or who inspired you to start your business?
I come from a long line of craftspeople, artists, and entrepreneurs. It seemed fitting to do the same myself.

What is your indulgence?
Shopping.

How do you spend your free time?
With what little free time I have, I like doing things that are not work related. I especially like spending time at the beach with my dog.

Where is your favorite place to go with your girlfriends?
I love shopping at the Wrenthem Village Outlets and making a whole day of it.

Photos by Janel Robertson

FIDDLEHEAD

24 Front St, Salem, 978.745.0008
fiddlehead-flowers.com, Twitter: @fiddleheadsalem

Creative. Fresh. Unique.
Fiddlehead is a European-style flower shop. Using your ideas, they will create an
exquisite floral feast for the eyes. Priding themselves on elegant simplicity, Fiddlehead
offers premium flowers, unique containers, and exceptional service and design.

Katherine Morse

Q and A

People may be surprised to know...
How many different items we carry. Our motto is, "always changing ... always fun!" The more you stop in, the less you miss! And in nice weather, we have the *best* sale bins going.

What is your indulgence?
I love buying nice gifts for people. It really is just as fun to give as it is to receive.

Where is your favorite place to go with your girlfriends?
Fenway Park.

What do you CRAVE? In business? In life?
Balance and happiness ... and to have the girls I work with never leave! They are the biggest asset I have.

THE FLAT OF THE HILL

60 Charles St, Boston, 617.619.9977
flatofthehill.com

Fun. Stylish. Unique.
A fun gift boutique filled with something for everyone, the flat of the hill offers
beautiful handbags at all price points, fun jewelry for all ages, bath and body
products, addictive candles and perfumes, cookbooks, great food, the most sought-
after baby items, and a famous selection of wood signs and pillows.

Photos by Kristina Young Photography

FLAUNT

617.714.5120
flauntitgirl.com, Twitter: @flauntitgirl

Fashionable. Valuable. Classy.
Flaunt is an online designer accessory consignment and resale boutique. Flaunt's goal is to enable women to shop consignment and resale with the same satisfaction of shopping at a high-end designer boutique. Flaunt is a shopping destination where customer service and integrity are the utmost priority, selling only authentic items and guaranteeing satisfaction.

Jenn Nash

Q and A

What are your most popular products or services?
Flaunt ladies love their handbags!
Shoes are a close second.

People may be surprised to know...
Every item purchased comes wrapped in tissue paper, is sealed with a Flaunt thank-you sticker, and includes a hand-written thank-you note.

What or who inspired you to start your business?
I surround myself with exceptional entrepreneurial people who have encouraged me for years to start my own business.

What do you CRAVE? In business? In life?
Learning about new areas of business, people, cultures ... as long as I am learning, I'm happy!

Who is your role model or mentor?
Spirited, successful business people. You can see the zest and passion for their business in their entire being. They're invigorating!

FLOCK

274 Shawmut Ave, Boston, 617.391.0222
flockboston.com, Twitter: @flockboston

Whimsical. Bohemian. Laid-back.
Flock is a whimsical neighborhood boutique where both mothers and daughters can shop a mix of laid-back California lines and hard-to-find brands. Tucked away on Shawmut Ave in the historic South End, Flock carries women's ready-to-wear accessories, jewelry, and shoes.

Photos by Leigh Smyth of Oh Snap! photography

Danielle and Lisa Kupsc

 Q and A

What are your most popular products or services?
Our eco-friendly line, Stewart + Brown, has had a
great response from our customers, as well as our
100 percent reclaimed metal jewelry line, Alkemie.

What or who inspired you to start your business?
Each other! We really wanted to have a store
where mothers and daughters could shop
together and both find something special.

Who is your role model or mentor?
Lisa's late husband (Danielle's dad)
was our biggest inspiration. He was
a successful entrepreneur who truly
believed in following your dreams.

What do you CRAVE? In business? In life?
In business, we hope to continue to
bring fresh products to our customers. In
life, we hope to surround ourselves with
positive people and experiences.

FORTY WINKS

56 JFK St, Cambridge, 617.492.9100
shopfortywinks.com, Twitter: @fortywinkshs

Relaxing. Cheerful. Feminine.
Forty Winks, located in charming Harvard Square, specializes in providing its clientele with quality lingerie and exceptional customer service. Owners Rachel Wentworth and Meredith Donaldson delight their customers with their light, airy store stocked with underpinnings to fit any occasion. Whether you're looking for comfortable, everyday pieces or something special, Forty Winks puts the fun into shopping for your undies.

Meredith Donaldson
and Rachel Wentworth

Q and A

What are your most popular products or services?
Bra fittings, obviously! Also, our Wish List
Program, which gives friends and significant
others a helpful framework when buying gifts.

What or who inspired you to start your business?
Friends and family who continued to complain
about the lack of lingerie options in our
area. We always knew we would open a
store together, and one day, the concept
of a lingerie boutique just clicked. We fell
totally in love with lingerie along the way.

**What business mistake have you
made that you will not repeat?**
When we were looking for a space, we got hung
up on little details, such as whether we were at
street level. It really set us back at first, but we
ended up taking a space with steps, and now our
customers say they love the privacy of the store.

What is your indulgence?
The clothes we wear over our lingerie!

What or who inspired you to start your business?

" My mother, also an entrepreneur, has taught me that I can make my craziest dreams come true."

Brett Mentuck of Mighty Aphrodite
Maternity Consignment

Aimee Lombardi Peabody

Q and A

People may be surprised to know...
The boutique carries designers one cannot find anywhere else in the United States. FRENCH + ITALIAN has been featured in *The Boston Globe*, *LUCKY Magazine*, Condé Nast's traveler's blog, Katy Elliott's blog, and *Northshore Magazine*. In three years of business, we have earned two "Best of ..." awards.

What or who inspired you to start your business?
The loss of my hero, my father. I realized that life is too short to be *doing* a job. I wanted to be *loving* my job.

Where is your favorite place to go with your girlfriends?
OTTO for lunch in New York.

FRENCH + ITALIAN

129 Washington St, Marblehead, 781.639.5129
frenchitalian.com

Luxurious. Imported. Minimal.
Owner Aimee Lombardi Peabody created FRENCH + ITALIAN in 2007. She brings
to you thoughtfully edited European apparel and accessories. As you shop, she
hopes you feel, if only for a few moments, like you're in Paris or Milan.

Photos by Renee Trichilo

Melissa Bennett

What are your most popular products or services?
Women come to French Dressing for the personal service and the expertise of our bra fitters. Popular lines include Aubade, Cosabella, Eberjey, and Le Mystere.

People may be surprised to know...
Most women are wearing the wrong bra size!

What or who inspired you to start your business?
My fiancé, Jack. When we first met, I was a retail manager and visual merchandiser. I loved what I did but was not crazy about the big corporate culture. Jack asked me many times what my dream in life was, and without hesitation, I always said I wanted to own my own boutique. When the opportunity to purchase French Dressing presented itself, I jumped on the chance with the encouragement and support of Jack.

FRENCH DRESSING

49 River St, Boston, 617.723.4YOU (617.723.4968)
frenchdressinglingerie.com, Twitter: @FrenchDressing1

Beautiful. Sexy. Confident.
French Dressing is an upscale lingerie boutique in Boston's exclusive Beacon Hill. One street over from busy Charles Street, French Dressing offers a quiet and intimate setting to try on some sweet, sexy lingerie. Whether you are in the mood to slip into something comfortable or something seductive, French Dressing is the place to shop! Bra fittings available.

GERI COSTANZA MASSAGEWORKS, INC.

781.631.4030
gericostanzamassage.com

Therapeutic. Healing. De-stressing.
Geri Costanza is one of the pioneers of massage and bodywork in Boston and surrounding communities. Blending the art and science of wellness, she applies her unique and proven method of unraveling and aligning muscles to treat clients for sports injuries, pain, and preventative-aging symptoms. Geri's approach increases strength endurance and flexibility in a soothing environment. She is a benchmark for therapeutic muscle care.

Geri Costanza

Q and A

What are your most popular products or services?
Alleviating tension and aligning muscles to improve the movement and strength of muscles and joints, head to toe. Appointments can be scheduled seven days per week, evenings as well, and gift certificates are available.

What or who inspired you to start your business?
An epiphany that my touch was a comfort and a way of listening, acknowledging, and communicating.

How do you spend your free time?
With friends and family, enjoying the outdoors, photographing nature, gardening, learning about nutrition, listening to music, contemplating curiosities, and researching questions regarding my work.

What is your indulgence?
Time to wonder and wander—especially an ocean walk at sunrise or an evening walk immersed in the scents of nature.

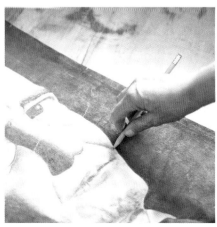

Joanna Howell-Giraud

 Q and A

What are your most popular products or services?
Exclusive Kérastase, Luzern Pure Cosmeceuticals, and Bio Ionic hair dryers.

People may be surprised to know...
I adore the opera!

What is your indulgence?
Yummy food, good wine, and British mysteries.

What do you CRAVE? In business? In life?
Smooth sailing and balance.
Enjoying what I love to do.

Who is your role model or mentor?
My mother, whom I could never do without.

What or who inspired you to start your business?
Beth Minardi, a world-famous colorist.

GIRAUD STUDIO

169 Bay Road, South Hamilton, 978.468.3202
giraudsalon.com

Luxurious. Professional. Elegant.
Award-winning former Newbury St. owner Joanna Howell-Giraud, along with her
husband, Omar Giraud, and colleague, Corey Melisi, welcome you to share their
passion for natural color and classic cutting techniques. Kérastase exclusive, Giraud
Studio has been described by clients as a quiet respite. From the cappuccino to the
blowdry, you are made to feel special. Giraud Studio is the ultimate retreat.

Photos by Leise Jones

What are your most popular products or services?
The Baby Tee and Capri Pant outfit is so versatile. The tank and thong combo make a cute bachelorette gift.

What or who inspired you to start your business?
My girlfriends! I had T-shirts made as favors for a girls'-night party I hosted. They were an instant hit!

Who is your role model or mentor?
My mother put herself through college and grad school, and had a successful career, all while raising us by herself.

What do you CRAVE? In business? In life?
Success and happiness. Doing something I believe in. This is true for both my business and personal life.

Hilary Glynn

GOOD WIFE

617.699.3724
goodwifeonline.com, Twitter: @goodwifeonline

Comfortable. Sexy. Unique.
Good Wife apparel is made for the woman who "does it all"—perfect for going
to the gym, running errands, or relaxing on the couch with a good book. Made
from the highest-quality cotton, the garments are extremely comfortable and
sexy. All of the pieces feature the adorable, conversation-starting Good Wife
logo, and are hand-embellished to make them as unique as you are.

GOODNESS GRACIOUS, LLC

goodnessgracioustreats.com, Twitter: @goodnssgracious

Healthy. Benevolent. Fearless.
Goodness Gracious makes all-natural dog treats and supplies, and donates 51 percent
of profits to animal shelters in communities where products are sold. The Hula Lula
jerky and wheat-free cookies include only human-grade ingredients found in your
own kitchen. The K#9 Cologne repels ticks naturally using essential oils. Goodness
Gracious products are sold in premium markets, cafés, pet boutiques, and online.

Photos by Renee Trichilo

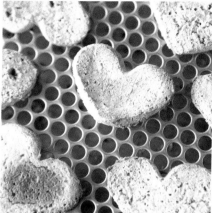

Amy Renz-Havens

Q and A

What is your indulgence?
Woodland walks with my pups (Gracie and Lula),
beach yoga, open-ocean slaloming, and dark
chocolate–covered strawberries for breakfast.

What or who inspired you to start your business?
Gracie and Lula—in one of those first
kiss moments, when your heart flutters
and you are forever changed.

People may be surprised to know...
Doing the right thing feels good. Five to seven
million pets land in shelters every year and
three to four million (60 percent of dogs and
70 percent of cats) are euthanized simply as a
result of overcrowding and limited resources.

What do you CRAVE? In business? In life?
To wag my tail, sniff everything, run
fast, love openly, and rub every belly
offered to me. Life is short!

Laurence
Howard

 Q and A

What or who inspired you to
start your business?
When my son was younger, I wanted a job
that worked with his schedule. Starting my
own business proved to be the best way to
accomplish this *and* do something I loved.

People may be surprised to know...
My name is not Grace!

Who is your role model or mentor?
My old nursery school teacher, Judy Scott,
formerly of Heeltapper Antiques. She is a
woman of great professional integrity who
enjoyed her work and always had time
to answer a question or offer advice and
encouragement as I started my business.

What is your indulgence?
A few classic pieces of clothing each season,
decorating and design books, and fudge.

GRACE SALES CO.

185 Pleasant St, Marblehead, 781.631.0046
gracesalesco.com

Affordable. Eclectic. Friendly.
Grace Sales Co. is a great place to find something unexpected, fine, and fun for your home, yourself, or for a gift. Traditional, mid-century and other styles are mixed in decorative vignettes, which include antique furniture, nautical artwork, '40s jewelry, Danish pottery, textiles, and more. Store inventory changes daily, so check in often! Grace Sales Co. also offers downsizing services.

Photos by Nina Gallant

HABIT

703 E Broadway, Boston, 617.269.1998
habitshop.com, Twitter: @habitshop

Stylish. Unique. Comfortable.
Habit is a small women's clothing and accessories boutique that caters to the young
professional. They offer great prices, quality merchandise, and a diverse selection of
jewelry and accessories. Owners Leila Moore and Pam Santorelli strive to offer great
customer service and clothing that will make you want to come back, even just to say
"hi." They also offer personal shopping services and closet-revamp sessions.

Photos by Leigh Smyth of Oh Snap! photography

Leila Moore and Pam Santorelli

 Q and A

People may be surprised to know...
Habit offers unique, affordable clothing
and accessories for any budget.
We won't break the bank.

What or who inspired you to start your business?
Each other. We have been fortunate enough
to work in the fashion business and learn
from many talented people. Our love and
commitment to what we do inspires us daily.

How do you spend your free time?
With family and friends, relaxing, traveling,
and going to the beach in the summer.

What is your indulgence?
Dinners out with friends, travel,
and Target shopping sprees!

HALEY'S WINES & SPIRITS

112 Washington St, Marblehead, 781.631.0169
haleyswine.com, Twitter: @haleyswine

Service-centric. Eclectic. Genuine.
Located in historic downtown Marblehead, Haley's Wines & Spirits features delicious boutique, sustainable, and organic wines from producers around the globe, as well as a diverse selection of local, craft, organic, gluten-free, and imported beers. (They also have a super selection of the usual fare). They also offer a wide variety of cool bar gadgets, accessories, giftware, and funky hostess gifts.

Julie Vinette

Q and A

What are your most popular products or services?
California Chardonnay, big Syrah, and Cabernet Sauvignon, specialty rums, and anything organic.

People may be surprised to know...
I am also an artist and member of the Bromfield Gallery in Boston.

What business mistake have you made that you will not repeat?
Purchasing an over-priced, dinosaur of a credit-card processing system. What was I thinking?

What is your indulgence?
Shoes, glorious shoes!

Where is your favorite place to go with your girlfriends?
Boston's South End on "First Fridays" for the art, the food, and people-watching.

83

Who is your role model or mentor?

"Coco Chanel. She was the ultimate game changer. People are still trying to catch up to her."

Bridget M. Riley of Boston Skin Solutions

HANDS OF TIME

617.359.6865
handsoftimeconcierge.com, Twitter: @pairofhands

Organized. Energetic. Creative.
Hands of Time provides much-needed support to busy individuals and businesses in Boston. Acting as your personal concierge, they can manage all your personal, household, and business needs, giving you more time to focus on what you enjoy. Services range from personal shopping or event planning, to pet sitting, plus an array of everyday tasks and one-off requests.

Carolyn Kraut

Q and A

What are your most popular products or services?
Our services are so diverse, but it's the everyday tasks that keep home and life humming that get requested the most. These include pet care, gift shopping, and arranging for home repairs.

People may be surprised to know...
We will take on any task, as long as it's ethical and legal.

What or who inspired you to start your business?
This business was a "light bulb moment" in my life. I needed a change, and while pondering my next move, I read about the use of a personal concierge. I already had a part-time pet-sitting business and thought the two concepts had synergy, would play to my strengths, and provide the variety I craved, while allowing me do all the things I love to do.

How do you spend your free time?
Reading, taking pictures, going to museums, and checking out local events.

Q and A

What are your most popular products or services?
Our cookie and brownie assortments are most popular because you can sample some of each!

People may be surprised to know...
We create centerpieces (filled with our gourmet sweets!) that double as favors for weddings, showers, and other celebrations.

What or who inspired you to start your business?
My goal was to create a high quality, handcrafted, unique gift that provided an alternative to flowers.

What is your indulgence?
Checking out new bakeries (and sampling, of course!)

Susan George

HARVARD SWEET BOUTIQUE

888.5.SWEETS (888.579.3387)
harvardsweetboutique.com, Twitter: @harvardsweets

Whimsical. Unique. Gourmet.
Harvard Sweet Boutique is an online gourmet baking company founded in 2007 by Sue George, and it has quickly established itself as a premier Internet gift retailer. Harvard Sweet Boutique's attention to detail extends from the product to the packaging. Baked goods are made-to-order in small batches from scratch using all-natural, premium ingredients, and are handsomely packaged in whimsically unique gift boxes.

HELENA'S

397 Massachusetts Ave, Arlington, 781.483.3055
helenasofarlington.com, Twitter: @helenasboutique

Colorful. Pretty. Stylish.
Helena's is a boutique featuring pretty, stylish, wearable clothes. The store was
built on the philosophy that a put-together look is easier to obtain than many
busy women think. Helena's offers a collection of colorful women's apparel,
accessories, maternity clothing, and shoes. The shop features unique separates
for everyday-wear chosen for their style, versatility, and affordable prices.

Katherine Venzke

Q and A

What are your most popular products or services?
We are experts at finding great separates to build
a competent wardrobe. Our customers love that.

People may be surprised to know...
The store is named after my daughter,
who was 2 years old when I opened.

What is your indulgence?
Our family cabin in Maine.

Where is your favorite place to
go with your girlfriends?
Sofra in Watertown for a long breakfast
and great conversation.

What do you CRAVE? In business? In life?
Balance and creativity topped off
with a great, bold necklace.

Before

After

Before

Cathy Moretti

Q and A

What are your most popular
products or services?
Residential real estate staging and design.

People may be surprised to know...
We have more than 4,000 square feet of
inventory, including many custom pieces.

What or who inspired you to
start your business?
The need for properties to be furnished
uniquely and not cookie-cutter.

What business mistake have you
made that you will not repeat?
Chintz ... Only kidding, it does have its place!

Where is your favorite place to
go with your girlfriends?
Anywhere we choose for our monthly girls'
lunch, as long as we're all together!

HOUSE BLEND, INC.
STAGING AND DESIGN

617.970.9001
house-blend.com

Innovative. Proven. Creative.

House Blend has set the standard for staging interiors since 2005. They are a full-service, value-add partner offering a unique approach of blending the architecture of your property with furniture and design elements to produce the most welcoming setting for clients. They take pride in their projects and hope that you will choose to add House Blend to your marketing team.

After

Photos by Leise Jones

Q and A

Alison Barnard

People may be surprised to know...
The average woman owns eight pairs of jeans!

What or who inspired you to
start your business?
A love of fashion and clothing prompted
me to work part-time at a small boutique. I
noticed that women love to buy jeans, but
not all jeans are made for all women. In order
to provide great service, you need to have
a broad selection for a variety of bodies!

Who is your role model or mentor?
My parents, Chet and Cynthia.

Where is your favorite place to
go with your girlfriends?
Dinner at Neptune Oyster in the North
End, or drinks on the roof deck at Fiore
in the summer. Also, there is nothing
better than going out dancing with the
girls at the Middlesex in Cambridge.

IN-JEAN-IUS

441 Hanover St, Boston, 617.523.5326
injeanius.com, Twitter: @injeaniusboston

TWILIGHT

12 Fleet St, Boston, 617.523.8008
twilightboutique.com, Twitter: @twilightboutiqu

Service-oriented. Stylish. Select.
In-jean-ius is centered on the one must-have clothing item for women: the perfect-fitting pair of jeans. The store is stocked to accommodate the many body types and personalities women have, and offers tops and accessories to complete your look. Twilight, meanwhile, focuses on style staples that take you from day to night for any type of occasion.

ISIS PARENTING

Arlington Center, 397 Massachusetts Ave, Arlington
Brookline Village, 2 Brookline Pl, Brookline
Needham/Newton, 110 Second Ave, Needham
The Shops at Prudential Center, 800 Boylston St, Boston
781.429.1500
isisparenting.com, Twitter: @isis_parenting

Sincere. Supportive. Informative.
Isis Parenting has quickly become Boston's most trusted and talked about resource for
new families, from pregnancy to pre-school. By operating community-based centers
that combine expert-led classes with specialty retail products, Isis has built a vibrant
and supportive environment that transcends the typical consumer experience.

Photos by Melissa Ostrow

Johanna Myers McChesney

 Q and A

What or who inspired you to start your business?
Becoming a parent can be really
challenging. We wanted to create a
resource to help make it more fun.

Who is your role model or mentor?
The unbelievably devoted employees at
Isis who inspire me to give the company
every ounce of energy I have.

What business mistake have you
made that you will not repeat?
I don't even know where to start. Mistakes
are many and the only real way to learn.

What do you CRAVE? In business? In life?
Deep connections with people. Meaningful
engagement with others is what life is
about. The rest of the stuff is just filler.

Janet Barsanti

Q and A

What are your most popular
products or services?
Helping women update their wardrobes with
personal attention to fit, fashion, and style.

People may be surprised to know...
J. Mode won "Best of North
Shore" the last two years!

What or who inspired you to
start your business?
I realized what I wanted to do the
rest of my life while walking the
cobblestoned streets of Salem.

Who is your role model or mentor?
Gail Fairfield, once my boss, now my friend
and advisor. Her can-do attitude, honesty,
and sincere interest in others inspire me.

J. MODE

17 Front St, Salem, 978.744.7007
jmodefashions.com, Twitter: @jmodefashions

Chic. Sophisticated. Fashion-forward.
J. Mode is a chic, contemporary clothing boutique located on Salem's historic cobblestoned Front Street. J. Mode's selections feature trendy denim and sexy cocktail dresses and everything in between. Owner Janet Barsanti spends endless hours putting together different collections to ensure the store has a fresh, cohesive assortment of the highest quality. J. Mode features designers from all over the world, always pushing the edge of fashion.

Photos by Leigh Smyth of Oh Snap! photography

Q and A

What are your most popular products or services?
The Design Session is the most popular service. It's an affordable few hours of brainstorming and easy solutions—a great jump-start to any design project!

People may be surprised to know...
With only a few quick changes, any room can be transformed. Rearranging furniture, painting, or adding accents can easily pull a space together.

How do you spend your free time?
I love having everyone over for a big dinner party, and if it is on the deck, even better!

What do you CRAVE? In business? In life?
Longevity in business, with the ability to continue seeing the happiness on clients' faces when their unveiled room is what they imagined it could be. Fantastic!

Julieann Covino

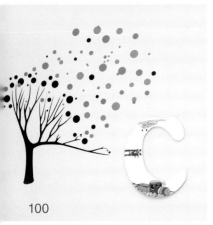

JACE INTERIORS

jaceinteriors.com, Twitter: @creategirl

Affordable. Creative. Inspiring.
Jace Interiors is a leading design group that works with you to make the home of your dreams a reality. Incorporating new and emerging styles, or keeping a more traditional approach, they create a brand-new room or design with your current pieces. They welcome both one room projects and entire house projects. Their motto: "Your Home, Your Style, My Assistance."

Photos by Leigh Smyth of Oh Snap! photography

JEAN THERAPY

524 Commonwealth Ave, Boston, 617.266.6555
jean-therapy.com, Twitter: @jeantherapy

Knowledgeable. Authentic. Gratifying.
Jean Therapy provides Boston with a customer service-oriented one-stop shop for
purchasing premium quality men's and women's jeans from companies that they love
and believe in, some of which can't be found anywhere else in Boston. Jean Therapy's
mission is to be an enjoyable, therapeutic, fun, and fulfilling shopping experience.

Leah Eckelberger

Q and A

What are your most popular products or services?
People come to us for our customer service. The staff goes through at least three months of jeans training.

What or who inspired you to start your business?
I've always had trouble finding jeans for my own body. On top of that, I never found a jean place in Boston that was both honest and nonexclusive.

What is your indulgence?
I'm lactose intolerant but adore all things dairy!

What do you CRAVE? In business? In life?
Love, passion, empowerment, and respect. I seek those things in all aspects of my life, including my business. I hope that when I'm 90 years old, I'm still helping people find amazing jeans at Jean Therapy!

Who is your role
model or mentor?

" *My grandmother
is very level-
headed, low-key,
and doesn't judge.
That is hard to
achieve. She also
plays a lot of poker
and forwards
me dirty jokes.* "

Tiffany Gaddis of She

Lauri Meizler

 Q and A

Who is your role model or mentor?
Dr. Mark Hyman, author of *Ultrametabolism*, taught me how the elimination of high allergen foods can help us optimize our metabolism, prevent disease, and lose weight. Sally Kravich, a natural health expert, who first taught me the importance of following a high alkaline diet. My mother inspired me to have healthy, balanced eating habits.

What business mistake have you made that you will not repeat?
Operating like an entrepreneur instead of a businessperson.

What is your indulgence?
Pulpcakes, one of the most delicious and healthiest baked goods ever made! Think of an incredibly moist muffin, but even better. Kids *love* pulpcakes.

JOOS LLC

617.571.5101
drinkjoos.com, Twitter: @organicJOOS

Empowering. Vibrant. Strengthening.
JOOS LLC is an integrated nutrition and lifestyle business that teaches people how to lead a balanced, vibrant, and healthy life. Offerings include: JOOS Delivery (local delivery of fresh, organic juices), JOOS Cleanse (a guided organic supplemented with lifestyle counselor support), JOOS Lifestyle (nutrition and wellness counseling), and Pulpcakes (gluten-free, vegan muffins/loaves that are made from JOOS' pulp).

Photos by Leise Jones

Jude Stearns

Q and A

What are your most popular products or services?
Haircuts, color services, Sebastian salon products, DevaCurl, Dermalogica, Alterna, Bumble and bumble, and keratin treatments.

People may be surprised to know...
We can do *anything*, from the most basic cut to elaborate color work.

Who is your role model or mentor?
Vidal Sassoon.

What business mistake have you made that you will not repeat?
I've never come across an issue I can't fix.

How do you spend your free time?
With my 6-year-old son, Gus—he's the love of my life!

JUDY JETSON, INC.

1765 Massachusetts Ave, Cambridge, 617.354.2628
judyjetson.com, Twitter: @judyjetsonsalon

Progressive. Industrial. Eclectic.
Judy Jetson, Inc. has been a staple in the hair scene for 35 years. Owner Jude Stearns started her business at only 29, rolling coins to pay for the first month's rent. Acting as her only employee for a full year as she started, she's now gone from one stylist to a 20-piece working family. Jude is proud to be a self-made businesswoman.

KEN ROTHWELL'S CUSTOM CATERING

978.825.0200
rothwellcatering.com

KEN'S KICKIN CHICKEN

7 Franklin St, Salem, 978.825.0200
kenskickinchicken.com

Professional. Efficient. Fun.
At Ken Rothwell's Custom Catering, the goal is to make your event the best it can be! Menus are designed to fit clients' taste and themes, with attention to detail and quality. Rothwell's is active in the local community Rotary and Chamber of Commerce. The theme at Rothwell's is "food is love," and they love to share that ideal with customers and neighbors.

Cris E. Ingemi

Q and A

What are your most popular products or services?
Our chicken pot pies and events.

People may be surprised to know...
This is a second career for me.

What or who inspired you to start your business?
My partner, Ken Rothwell.

Who is your role model or mentor?
My grandmother who was the
strongest woman I've ever met.

What business mistake have you
made that you will not repeat?
Not following my gut instincts!

How do you spend your free time?
With my 10-year-old son.

What do you CRAVE? In business? In life?
Happiness, fulfillment, success, and
being the best "me" I can be.

111

KICKASS CUPCAKES

378 Highland Ave, Somerville, 617.628.2877
kickasscupcakes.com, Twitter: @kickasscupcakes

Whimsical. Fresh. Kickass.
Kickass Cupcakes is Boston's first cupcake bakery. Their artisanal bakers use only the best all-natural ingredients and bake from scratch every day. Featuring more than a dozen different flavors, an ever-changing variety of cupcake flavors, and a unique spin on the cupcake, Kickass Cupcakes is maximum cupcake satisfaction guaranteed, with no fork required.

Sara Ross

 Q and A

What are your most popular products or services?
Cupcakes and cupcake towers, especially
with mini cupcakes, which are popular for
weddings, parties, and all sorts of occasions.

What or who inspired you to start your business?
Once we came up with the name Kickass
Cupcakes, there was no turning back,
especially since there were no cupcake
bakeries in Boston at the time.

What is your indulgence?
I love getting lost in a good book, and I'll
spend a whole stolen afternoon reading
a page-turner from start to finish.

Who is your role model or mentor?
An incredible chef I worked for in Los
Angeles at Campanile and Lucques
restaurants, Suzanne Goin.

Kristine Irving

 Q and A

What are your most popular
products or services?
Our lotus nesting bowls—exclusive
to Koo de Kir—sell so quickly! We
ship them all over the world.

People may be surprised to know...
Koo de Kir is really quite accessible in
terms of price points. I work hard to find
a range of products that are not only well
designed, but that also represent the idea
of value. I want my customers to grow with
me. If $20 is all you have today, you can find
something beautiful, and when you have
$200 down the road, we'll be right here.

Where is your favorite place to
go with your girlfriends?
I love Neptune Oyster in the North End
and Dali in Somerville. Both are great
spots for girl talk over drinks and food.

KOO DE KIR

65 Chestnut St, Boston, 800.944.2591
Koo de Kir Design Studio: 45 River St, Boston, 800.944.2591
koodekir.com, Twitter: @koodekir

Sexy. Stylish. Attainable.
Koo de Kir is a retail home boutique and interior design firm specializing in
stylish, carefully edited furnishings and accessories. They have been striking the
hearts of Bostonians and beyond since opening in 1997. The name is a phonetic
rendering of the expression *coup de coeur*, or "a strike to the heart."

Photos by Leigh Smyth of Oh Snap! photography

115

Nicole Cronin

 Q and A

What are your most popular products or services?
Private shopping parties with a 20 percent discount, complimentary wine, and hors d'oeuvres; unique jewelry collections from Europe and Asia; and a wide range of designer denim.

People may be surprised to know...
Almost everything in our boutique is under $100.

What or who inspired you to start your business?
Combining my love of fashion and travel, Ku De Ta enabled me to bring global fashion trends to Boston.

Who is your role model or mentor?
Coco Chanel. Her elegance and simplicity was fashionable, yet timeless.

KU DE TA

663 E Broadway, S Boston, 617.269.0008
kudetaboston.com

Unique. Fashion-forward. Stylish.
Ku De Ta is a fashionable women's clothing and accessories boutique located in vibrant South Boston. This one-stop-shop offers an ever-changing inventory of unique, fashion-forward trends. The knowledgeable, low-pressure sales staff can always help you find something perfect for that special occasion, or just add a distinctive piece to your wardrobe.

Photos by Leigh Smyth of Oh Snap! photography

Lisa J.B. Peterson

What are your most popular products or services?
We specialize in fee-only financial planning for young professional couples and individuals. We offer several different customizable service plans.

People may be surprised to know...
The highest cited reason for divorce is financial conflict. Our financial counseling service teaches couples to communicate about money.

What or who inspired you to start your business?
Previously, I worked with older clients. I always knew high-quality planning could make a huge difference to younger people.

Who is your role model or mentor?
My grandfather was an entrepreneur and inventor. I was always fascinated by his stories about creating something completely new.

LANTERN FINANCIAL LLC

50 Franklin Street, 3rd Floor
Boston, MA 02110
Phone: 617-482-2700
Fax: 617-482-2710
lisa@lantern-financial.com

Lisa J.B. Peterson, CFP®
President and Senior Financial Planner

www.lantern-financial.com
www.lantern-financial.blogspot.com

LANTERN FINANCIAL, LLC

50 Franklin St, 3rd Floor, Boston, 617.482.2700
lantern-financial.com, Twitter: @lisalantern

Young. Inspirational. Bright.
Lantern Financial is a financial planning firm exclusively dedicated to helping young professionals and couples reach their goals and dreams. They believe that everyone can have the life they truly desire if they surround themselves with that which they love, and eliminate that which they do not value. Lantern especially inspires their clients toward success through their one-of-a-kind financial counseling programs.

Photos by Renee Trichilo

LAURA LANES SKIN CARE

242 Essex St, Salem, 978.741.8777
lauralanes.com

Friendly. Relaxing. Rejuvenating.
Laura Lanes Skin Care is a world-class bioelements skin-care salon specializing in facials, waxing, makeup, and massage therapy. They use and recommend salon-exclusive Mirabella makeup. Their friendly, licensed professionals are ready to help you relax and feel beautiful.

Laura Lanes

What are your most popular products or services?
Waxing and facial treatments.

People may be surprised to know...
I have been a licensed esthetician for 20 years.

What or who inspired you to start your business?
My husband, Scott, encouraged and helped
me to open my business seven years ago.

Who is your role model or mentor?
My father. He was a self-employed
auto mechanic most of his career.

What business mistake have you
made that you will not repeat?
Working too much! It's an ongoing struggle.

What is your indulgence?
Spa services! That's why I chose this field.
Facials, massage, pedicures—I love it all!

Laurie A. Mandato

 Q and A

What are your most popular
products or services?
My "Spotlight on You" VIP package. It offers
the best results in a short period of time.

People may be surprised to know...
Discovering your unique presence
is easier than you think.

What or who inspired you to
start your business?
I was inspired to create my life on my
terms, doing work that I love!

What is your indulgence?
Chocolate, champagne, and great shoes!

What business mistake have you
made that you will not repeat?
Allowing fear to stand in the way of
creating a life and business that I love.

LAURIEMANDATO.COM

781.771.7688
lauriemandato.com, Twitter: @lauriemandato

Empowering. Authentic. Stylish.
Laurie Mandato's philosophy isn't about bringing the pages of the latest fashion magazines to your closet. It's about figuring out who you are, what you're comfortable wearing, and what colors work for you, and then designing a wardrobe that represents your message. The right look with the right colors, fabrics, and tailoring can be an expression of, and an enhancement to, your inner light.

Photos by Renee Trichilo

Forty Winks photographed by Renee Trichilo

Where is your favorite place to go with your girlfriends?

" *Brunch. By the second mimosa, the dirt's been divulged, day-to-day crisis consulted, and we're laughing so hard we're in tears.* "

Jessica deGuardiola of 5s Public Relations

Leah Robins

Q and A

People may be surprised to know...
Hiring a good interior designer early in the design process to work alongside the architect and/or contractor is extremely important and beneficial to the client. Mistakes can be costly!

Who is your role model or mentor?
My mother. She is frugal, self-sufficient, and organized. Her environmental consciousness has been a foundation for my personal and professional lifestyle.

How do you spend your free time?
Exercising, gardening, and entertaining. My favorite exercise class is Core Fusion at Exhale in Boston.

What is your indulgence?
Spending 10 days alone each fall in Amagansett, Long Island, painting the landscape.

LEAH ROBINS DESIGNS

617.470.8688
leahrobinsdesigns.com

Thoughtful. Cohesive. Artistic.
Leah Robins Designs provides comfortable and functional interiors for every room of the home to reflect your sensibilities and lifestyle. Client inspiration is translated into rooms that are warm and peaceful with an artistic style. Completed projects are elegant and timeless!

127

Nicoletta Lyons

Q and A

What or who inspired you to
start your business?
My interest and work as a costume designer
inspired me to explore opportunities to expand
my vision into fashion and jewelry design.

People may be surprised to know...
I am also a fashion photo stylist.

Who is your role model or mentor?
My mother and grandmother were style
mavens and businesswomen. My mother
continues to mentor me and introduce
design ideas that I implement.

What do you CRAVE? In business? In life?
Passion, passion, passion. "There is no end.
There is no beginning. There is only the
infinite passion of life."—Federico Fellini.

LOLA'S URBAN VINTAGE

187 Harvard Ave, Allston, 617.254.5652
lolasurbanvintage.com

Chic. Edgy. Urban.
Lola's Urban Vintage is a retail boutique where one-of-a-kind accessories and cutting-edge fashion are offered at reasonable and affordable prices. Lola's combines vintage and nouveau to link the past to the present. Lola's is a mind-set where you can reveal your identity through the shadow of the past and the lens of the future.

Photos by Leigh Smyth of Oh Snap! photography

LOLAGRACEEVENTS

535 Albany St, Ste 200, Boston, 617.650.8823
lolagraceevents.com, Twitter: @lolagraceboston

Fearless. Reliable. Creative.
LolagraceEVENTS is a boutique event-planning firm that specializes in wedding planning for the anti-bride—brides looking to throw a party, not a bouquet. But it doesn't stop there! LolagraceEVENTS also specializes in nightlife event planning. Currently managing and producing the lolagraceLOLITAS, lolagraceEVENTS provides 360-degree event production and management services throughout the Boston area.

Main photo (this page), and top left and right photo (opposite page) by Kjeld Mahoney Photography; top middle photo (opposite page) by Josh Rubino Photography; portrait (opposite page) by Melissa Ostrow

Rachael Gross

 Q and A

What are your most popular products or services?
Nightlife entertainment that integrates
fashion, music, and philanthropy—
the lolagraceLOLITAS! And, of course,
wedding planning for the anti-bride.

People may be surprised to know...
Lolagrace is my alter ego.

What or who inspired you to start your business?
My nana. She accidently taught me to stop
dreaming and to start doing. So, I am doing.

How do you spend your free time?
Work is play and play is work. If I'm able to break
away from either of those two items, I spend
time snuggling with my two beautiful nephews.

What do you CRAVE? In business? In life?
The opportunity to entertain ...
in business and in life!

Sheri Gurock

Q and A

What are your most popular
products or services?
We are famous for stroller matchmaking.
We get to know our customers and help
them choose the perfect stroller. Stroller
test drives are encouraged, too.

People may be surprised to know...
A product has to be really good to earn a
spot on our shelves. In fact, manufacturers
often bring us new ideas and prototypes to
review. They know we'll be brutally honest
about whether they would make the cut.

Where is your favorite place to
go with your girlfriends?
I love the new Regal Beagle in Coolidge
Corner. It's got such a chic, fun vibe
with great food and drinks.

MAGIC BEANS

312 Harvard St, Brookline, 617.264.2326
361 Huron Ave, Cambridge, 617.300.0171
94 Derby St, Hingham, 781.749.2321
200 Linden St, Wellesley, 781.235.2120
mbeans.com, Twitter: @sherigurock

Friendly. Smart. Fun.
Magic Beans sells baby gear and toys for all ages. The comprehensive selection is carefully curated by parents who have been there, done that. Magic Beans has built a reputation for outstanding customer service and was named one of the "21 Best Baby Shops in America" by *Baby Bargains* in 2010. They have four Boston-area locations and an award-winning website.

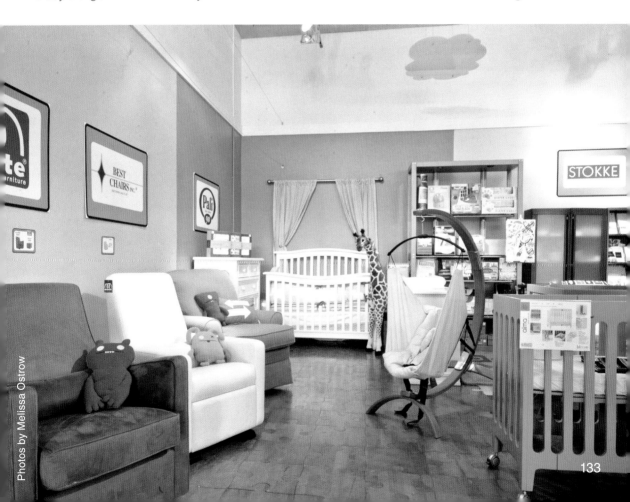

Photos by Melissa Ostrow

MARMALADE

695 Belmont St, Belmont, 617.484.0093
shopmarmalade.com

Eclectic. Creative. Stylish.
Marmalade is a jewel-box of a shop tucked away in a Belmont neighborhood. Featuring products by parent-company Curly Girl Design Studios, this colorful boutique has something for everyone: jewelry, candles, stationery, and gifts galore! With an artful and eclectic collection of products, a bright and colorful atmosphere, and a sweet dog on staff, you will find yourself returning often.

Q and A

Leigh Standley

People may be surprised to know...
Curly Girl Design Studios are located directly
beneath our Belmont location. The owner's dog is
a constant fixture and loves when children visit.

What or who inspired you to start your business?
We were searching for a perfect outlet for our
own product in the Boston area, and nothing
was exactly right, so we opened our own!

What business mistake have you
made that you will not repeat?
I have made many, and will try not to repeat
the bad ones, like impulsive hiring, or over-
buying. But, I really believe that making
them has strengthened the business.

Where is your favorite place to
go with your girlfriends?
Cape Cod for a long weekend. Big meals,
late mornings, and lots of sunshine.

135

Dava Muramatsu

Q and A

What are your most popular products or services?
Our approach is about creating an individual sense of style. Our carefully edited selections from the likes of Elm, Lilith, and Comme des Garçons express subtle opulence that inspires and speaks from within.

How do you spend your free time?
Creating my Nymph jewelry collection, cooking, photography, blogging, and practicing yoga.

What is your indulgence?
The beach, good Bordeaux, and sandalwood and lavender bubble baths.

What do you CRAVE? In business? In life?
Beauty, passion, and creativity. I thrive on the stimulation of the senses in both work and play. I always follow my passion, and inspire women to do the same in every aspect of life.

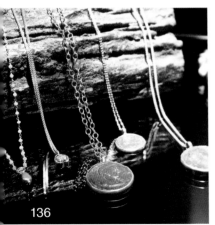

MATSU

259 Newbury St, Boston, 617.266.9707
matsuboston.com

Vibrant. Enriching. Stylish.
More than a boutique, Matsu is an oasis. Since 1995, Matsu has brought playful, sophisticated clothing and a seductive selection of jewelry and accessories to loyal customers from near and far. "I believe that an environment of beauty and reflection stirs the imagination and nourishes the soul. Matsu, and each hand-selected item in it, is testament to this."—Dava Muramatsu

MERRYFOXREALTY

224 Derby St, Salem, 978.740.0008
merryfoxrealty.com

Energy. Expertise. Fun.
The goal at MerryFoxRealty is to build on their strong foundation of market knowledge to provide the highest level of customer service and attention to detail, and to maximize technology to reach a widening market. They bring all of these components together to benefit each client. MerryFoxRealty is proud to be the leading real-estate team on the North Shore.

Photos by Renee Trichilo

Betsy Merry

Q and A

What or who inspired you to start your business?
My career began in real estate in a small boutique company. When we were acquired by a larger corporate real-estate firm, I went from sales to management. It was time to put my own brand on a real-estate company.

What business mistake have you made that you will not repeat?
I will never again work for a large real-estate corporation. Unfortunately, the large real-estate firms are run by accounts.

What is your indulgence?
Flowers, limoncello, and Creed Green Irish Tweed (I wear men's fragrances). After living in Italy when I was at Boston College, I learned to appreciate quality, not quantity. Don't save your best china for a special day. Make every day special. Live life with zest every day.

Brett Mentuck

Q and A

What are your most popular products or services?
We carry a wide range of jeans, dresses, and blouses, as well as business suits, bathing suits, and lots more.

People may be surprised to know...
I am a DONA birth doula, trained in labor support.

What or who inspired you to start your business?
My mother, also an entrepreneur, has taught me that I can make my craziest dreams come true.

What is your indulgence?
Sundresses. I can't get enough of cute, 1950s vintage sundresses. The more rickrack and flowers, the better.

MIGHTY APHRODITE
MATERNITY CONSIGNMENT

244 Essex St, Salem, 978.745.8900
mightyaphroditematernity.com

Stylish. Friendly. Affordable.
Mighty Aphrodite Maternity Consignment is devoted exclusively to the pregnant mama. They carry gently used maternity clothes designed to replace your pre-preggo clothes with a smokin' hot wardrobe that is sexy, stylish, and won't cripple you financially. They also carry new accessories like Bravado! bras and BellaBands.

Photos by Renee Trichilo

141

Brooke Garber and Stephanie Nist

People may be surprised to know...
Our staff is like a big family with
many of the girls having been with
us for more than three years!

What or who inspired you to
start your business?
Entrepreneurs at heart, we wanted to open
the dream store we longed to shop at.

Who is your role model or mentor?
Rachel Strules of "Sweet Lady Jane" in
Burlington, Vermont, took us in six years
ago and remains our mentor today.

Where is your favorite place to
go with your girlfriends?
Florida, California, and any country
where John Mayer is playing!

What do you CRAVE? In business? In life?
Happiness and joy for our

MINT JULEP

6 Church St, Cambridge, 617.576.6468
1302 Beacon St, Brookline, 617.232.3600
shopmintjulep.com

Fresh. Welcoming. Fun.
Mint Julep is a charming women's clothing boutique with locations in Brookline and
Cambridge, as well as Manhattan's Lower East Side. The neighborhood shops offer a wide
selection of clothing, jewelry, and accessories. Each piece is selected with thought and
love so you browse through a well-edited collection of favorites from many designers.

What business mistake
have you made that
you will not repeat?

" *Sharing ideas with
the naysayer. It
slows you down.* **"**

Chintra Kimkhnal of Orange Nail Studio

MOD BOSTON

184 Washington St, Dorchester, 617.265.0011
modboston.com, Twitter: @mod_boston

Contemporary. Unique. Trendy.
MOD Boston is a women's boutique offering upscale appeal, chic ambience, energetic vibe, and cutting-edge fashion. The boutique carries premium designer apparel with a focus also on the plus-size market. MOD Boston provides an inviting, charming atmosphere and affordable prices, providing customers a comfortable shopping experience.

Vanessa Targete

People may be surprised to know...
Our items are exclusive and fashion-forward.

What or who inspired you to start your business?
My brother, Patrick, co-founded MOD Boston.
I was inspired by his vision for the business
as well as my love of fashion.

Who is your role model or mentor?
My role models are my three older brothers
who continually encourage me to better my
business and myself. They are all successful
business owners and I model myself after them.

How do you spend your free time?
I spend my free time enjoying life with
my family and friends.

What is your indulgence?
To be honest, I love shopping for accessories—
anything to accessorize an outfit: shoes,
jewelry, a headpiece, a clutch...

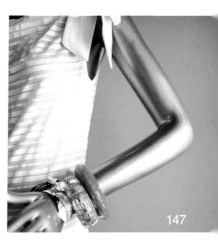

MODERN MILLIE VINTAGE & CONSIGNMENT SHOP

103 Washington St, Salem, 978.745.0231
41 Pleasant St, Newburyport, 978.961.1569
modernmillieshop.com

Stylish. Friendly. Fun.
Modern Millie Vintage & Consignment Shop specializes in affordable and trendy modern clothes as well as wearable vintage. In this award-winning store, you'll find racks of adorable dresses and cute separates including '70s maxis, '50s cocktail dresses, and modern designer jeans. Stop in for your own wardrobe renovation by Millie stylists!

Photos by Leigh Smyth of Oh Snap! photography

148

Christine Robidoux

 Q and A

What are your most popular products or services?
Vintage dresses spanning 1940 to
1970 in fun prints or bold solids.

Who is your role model or mentor?
My grandmother, the most stylish woman, who
made her own clothing and was always dressed
as well as any model in the magazines. She taught
me how to sew with vintage fabric when I was a
little girl and ignited the fashionable girl in me.

Where is your favorite place to
go with your girlfriends?
Wildhorse in Beverly.

What do you CRAVE? In business? In life?
Success. I am not speaking of monetary
success, but rather affecting people's lives
for the better and changing the canvas
of the towns Modern Millie settles in.

Lisa Johnson

Q and A

What are your most popular products or services?
Privates (one-on-one training) and trios (three clients and one instructor).

People may be surprised to know...
How quickly you feel the difference, often with just one session.

What or who inspired you to start your business?
A physical therapist who rehabilitated my knee and told me about Pilates. Once I tried it, I was hooked.

How do you spend your free time?
I love hanging with my friends, hula-hooping, or taking photos. I firmly believe that food is love. I cook a lot!

MODERN PILATES

1285 Beacon St, Brookline, 617.232.1010
1110 Great Plain Ave, Needham, 781.455.1121
154 Turnpike Road, Southborough, 508.460.8882
modernpilatesboston.com, Twitter: @modernpilates

Energizing. Graceful. Svelte.
Modern Pilates has been training clients since 1999. Their trainers are known for tough workouts and a sense of humor. They use Reformers and Cadillacs in their group classes—giving you a never-ending selection of more than 450 exercises to choose from! With Modern Pilates, you'll be red-carpet-ready for your next gala, and you can blast off that mummy tummy in no time flat.

Karen Fabbri

 Q and A

What or who inspired you to
start your business?
The other savvy, strong women business
owners in Beacon Hill who dared to
change the neighborhood 10 years ago.

Who is your role model or mentor?
My mother—who worked full-time, earned
a college degree at night, cared for two
kids, and modeled the important balance
between family, work, and self.

How do you spend your free time?
Playing with my children, sharing wine and
good food with my husband and friends, and
volunteering with organizations that move me.

What is your indulgence?
New Zealand Sauvignon blanc and
very expensive handbags.

MOXIE

51 Charles St, Boston, 617.557.9991
24 Church St, Wellesley, 781.235.1833
moxieboston.com, Twitter: @moxieboston

Vibrant. Feminine. Playful.
Boston's most-fashionable shoe and accessories aficionados feed their cravings at Moxie. Whether one is feeling feminine or fierce, Moxie's selection is always engaging, flirty, strong, and fabulous. With selections from top designers such as Tory Burch, Cynthia Vincent, Loeffler Randall, Foley & Corinna, Kooba, and Beirn, Moxie will create a look to make you the envy of your friends.

Photos by Leigh Smyth of Oh Snap! photography

MULBERRY ROAD

46 Gloucester St, Boston, 617.859.5861
mulberryroad.com

Whimsical. Unique. Stylish.
Located in a historic brownstone just off of famous Newbury Street, Mulberry
Road is an adorable baby boutique offering unique clothing, accessories, shoes,
toys, and books from American and European designers. Mulberry Road has a
wonderful customer base that depends on them for excellent customer service and
the perfect baby gift for any occasion, including complimentary gift wrap!

Sandy Nelson

Q and A

What are your most popular products or services?
We carry a layette line called Kissy Kissy, which is made of the softest cotton from Peru—perfect for bringing baby home. Our complimentary gift wrap is ideal for our busy customers.

People may be surprised to know...
We offer a stroller valet service. Customers just knock on the window and we assist them with lifting the stroller into the store. If something is out of stock, we can order it specifically for a customer—just ask. We feature an "outfit of the week" for 30 percent off the entire outfit.

What or who inspired you to start your business?
I purchased the store in 2005 after deciding that I wanted to change careers. Haven't looked back since! Love it!

What is your indulgence?
Vacations. I always have to research until I find the very best resort. Then, until the vacation, I try to rationalize why it is worth the money! It always is.

155

Dana Appel Young

 Q and A

What are your most popular products or services?
I recommend and personalize weight loss programs while also offering the latest in meal replacement shakes, natural health supplements, and weight loss and anti-aging products.

How do you spend your free time?
I spend time in the gym, running outside, and am an intenSati leader. I am a single mom with three beautiful children who keep me very busy as well.

What do you CRAVE? In business? In life?
Happiness, success, and the best of health, in business and in life. As I teach in my intenSati class, live a life you love in a body you love!

NEW DAY

8 Bartlett St, Marblehead, 781.389.0538
amazingnewday.com, Twitter: @amazingnewday

Motivating. Empowering. Amazing.
Do you want to lose weight, rev up your metabolism, feel stronger and more energized every day? NEW DAY owner Dana Appel Young is a certified health coach who offers personal health coaching and training. Let her simplify things for you and, at the very minimum, help set you on the path to a healthier, more amazing new you.

Main photo (this page), portrait, and top right photo (opposite page) by Renee Trichilo; top left photo (opposite page) by KBT PHOTOGRAPHY; top middle photo (opposite page) by IrinaPhotography

NOMAD

1741 Massachusetts Ave, Cambridge, 617.497.6677
nomadcambridge.com

Vibrant. Fresh. Irresistible.
NOMAD is Cambridge's original global store. For 22 years NOMAD has been a neighborhood corner shop with, personally selected jewelry, clothing, folk art, textiles, books, and wondrous objects that capture imagination. Their goal is to create a beautiful and inviting place to shop while keeping true to green and fair trade ideals.

Photos by Leise Jones

Deb Colburn

 Q and A

What are your most popular products or services?
Everyone loves our organic clothing
lines, our eclectic jewelry selection, and
unique gifts. We also have a repeat group
of people who have traveled the world
with us on many Art and Soul Tours.

Who is your role model or mentor?
Ruth Lechuga, a Mexican
anthropologist and photographer.

What business mistake have you
made that you will not repeat?
Straying from our ideals in an attempt to please
everyone. We have found our greatest success in
remaining true to our original business concept.

Where is your favorite place to
go with your girlfriends?
Rendezvous in Central Square.

Leigh Smyth

Who is your role model or mentor?
Fine artist Lyn Ostrov, and photographer
Joseph Hyde from Baltimore are
my mentors and role models.

What business mistake have you
made that you will not repeat?
Not checking the weather for a shoot
and nearly giving my camera a bath,
if it weren't for a trash bag.

How do you spend your free time?
Traveling, enjoying live music, and
spending time with friends.

Where is your favorite place to
go with your girlfriends?
The Good Life bar in Boston is the
best, hands down. The music is
loud, and the staff is friendly.

160

Photos by Leigh Smyth of Oh Snap! photography

OH SNAP!

www.itakeyourphotos.net

Sincere. Fun. Candid.
With a knack for capturing moments in their honesty, Leigh Smyth strives to express the subtle humanity and spontaneity of life before her lens. Her versatile background has taken her from posh nightclubs to fashion shoots. Leigh cultivates an intimate allure and ambiance in her multi-faceted subject matter.

OLIVIA BROWNING

20 City Square, Charlestown, 617.242.2299
oliviabrowning.com, Twitter: @oliviabrowning1

Gorgeous. Tangible. Unique.
Olivia Browning is a distinctive gift store with something for everyone from age 0 to 100!
Gourmet goods, bridal and baby registries, bags, bath and body products, jewelry, stationery,
pet-related items, tabletops and linens—they've got it all. They also offer event planning,
specializing in weddings. Come to Olivia Browning to really see the magic of customer service!

Photos by Melissa Ostrow

Abby Gray

 Q and A

People may be surprised to know...
There is nothing that we won't search for
if you want it. We'll always do our best to
accommodate our customers' wishes.

What or who inspired you to start your business?
My friends, family, and children. There was
nothing like it in our community. I had always
wanted to open a shop—a beautiful shop set
up like a French market—lots of everything!

What business mistake have you
made that you will not repeat?
Ordering too much of a good or bad
thing. A deal is not usually a deal!

What is your indulgence?
Probably a pedicure! I realize, as I get
older, that as long as my family is healthy
and happy, I don't need much else.

Where is your favorite place to go with your girlfriends?

"*Dancing! We don't do it often enough, but as I get older, I have noticed that a good night of dancing with the girls will cure just about any ailment.*"

Lauren Genatossio of Sarra

ORANGE NAIL STUDIO

950 Cummings Center, Ste 100X, Beverly, 978.922.3133
orangenailstudio.com

Vibrant. Polished. Empowering.
A next-generation nail salon, Orange Nail Studio provides familiar mani-pedi salon services, but with a twist (of orange). Customers are pampered with first-class treatments, high-end customer service, and quality finish in an environment that's sleek but cozy.

Q and A

Chintra Kimkhnal

What are your most popular products or services?
Our signature Orange Passion Pedicure. It's a vacation for your feet! This service focuses extra attention on nails and cuticles and provides special treatment for rough calluses and problem areas. A two-phase foot massage is then followed by a soothing hot towel treatment and our exclusive Orange Heel Therapy.

What business mistake have you made that you will not repeat?
Sharing ideas with the naysayer. It slows you down.

What is your indulgence?
Home-cooked meals. I don't like to cook, but love to eat. If your mom is cooking, count me in.

Where is your favorite place to go with your girlfriends?
Any place that has food. My friends and I are all very busy and it's the only way for us to downshift.

Jessica Good

Q and A

What are your most popular products or services?
Our customers love our soft jersey dresses, fold-up flats, silk eye masks, and weekend bags.

People may be surprised to know...
We're more than a travel store! We cater to women who want to be comfortable without sacrificing style.

What or who inspired you to start your business?
My on-the-go, travel-savvy friends and family motivated me to create a business to cater to their lifestyle.

What is your indulgence?
Coats. I love a great-fitting trench. It is worth the money, since you will have it forever.

PASSPORT

43 Brattle St, Cambridge, 617.576.0900
passportboutique.com, Twitter: @passportboutiqu

Contemporary. Comfortable. Jet-setting.
Passport is a contemporary travel boutique specializing in accessories, luggage, and comfy-chic apparel for the modern jet-setter. Passport carries women's clothing lines with easy-to-wear, packable styles, and practical, yet stylish accessories from laptop and cosmetic cases to carry-on bags and weekenders. We help customers achieve the best travel experience—even if that travel is just their daily commute.

Photos by Leigh Smyth of Oh Snap! photography

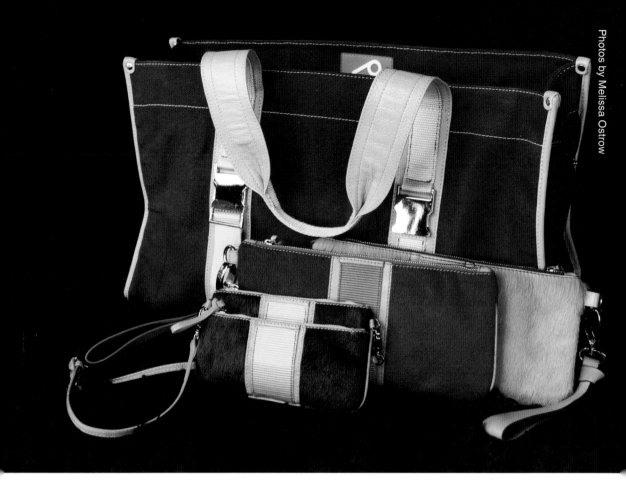

PLANK

50 Terminal St, Ste 311, Charlestown, 617.241.6900
plankdesigns.com, Twitter: @plankmatsnmore

Audacious. Artful. Sophisticated.
Plank's premium yoga mats and bags are made with superior quality and workmanship. Their striking eco-friendly yoga mats deliver high-performance functionality and are also pieces of commissioned art. Plank mats were conceived to stimulate thought and debate, both inside and outside the yoga studio, while their sharp accessories capture the "fun" in function. Their designs touch the audacious brilliance and spirited personality inside us all.

Doreen Hing

Q and A

What are your most popular products or services?
Our artistic yoga mats. Each image has several layers of reference that can be enjoyed by new-to-yoga and long-time practitioners alike. Plank's canvas bags and leather accessories are designed to serve multiple functions.

People may be surprised to know...
Before opening Plank, I was a footwear designer. Thus, I have a passion for accessories and fashion. Also, I love Plank's manufacturing partners in Asia who practice yoga, too, and, as a result, are vested in producing great quality yoga mats for us.

Who is your role model or mentor?
The Bob team from Bob's Your Uncle. They really are shining examples of a couple working and living their lifestyle together.

What is your indulgence?
I don't think I'll ever get over my love affair with shoes!

Allison Yee

What are your most popular products or services?
Our Closet Cure and Divine Intervention packages—a closet-editing session and a fun, focused shopping trip is the perfect combination.

People may be surprised to know...
I'm a bargain shopper at heart. I love the thrill of a discounted designer find and help my clients indulge in the same way!

What or who inspired you to start your business?
I'd been styling and shopping for my friends and family for years and always felt tremendously satisfied when they'd emerge looking chic and confident, so it was a logical leap.

POLISHED WARDROBE ADVISING

617.304.0449
polishedadvising.com, Twitter: @PolishedStyling

Imaginative. Inspired. Informative.
Polished Wardrobe Advising provides customized wardrobe styling and shopping services for individuals and groups to help them achieve confident, current looks based on their budgets, bodies, and lifestyles. Polished stylists equip their clients with key pieces of clothing and nuggets of knowledge to make chaotic closets, challenging mornings, and unproductive shopping trips a thing of the past!

Photos by Leigh Smyth of Oh Snap! photography

POLKA DOG BAKERY

256 Shawmut Ave, Boston, 617.338.5155
42 S St, Jamaica Plain, 617.522.1931
polkadog.com, Twitter: @polkadogbakery

Original. Innovative. Community-minded.
Polka Dog Bakery began in the heart of Boston's hip and historic South End. Founded as a tribute to a one-eyed rescue boxer, Pearl, the local dog hangout keeps Pearl's memory alive and embraces her spirit. All Polka Dog treats are baked fresh from scratch every day, using the finest ingredients. They can be found in quality shops around the globe.

Deborah Gregg

What are your most popular products or services?
Last year Polka Dog began making
Chicken Littles. They're bite-size, ideal for
training, and loaded with tasty chicken.

People may be surprised to know...
Dogs don't eat everything. Some do,
but many will turn up their nose at one
treat and gobble down another.

What or who inspired you to start your business?
A malnourished, elderly, one-eyed rescue
boxer named Pearl. She was an avid dancer.

What is your indulgence?
A slow-cooked bowl of chili, a loaf
of salt-encrusted homemade bread,
and a full-bodied red wine.

What do you CRAVE? In business? In life?
Health, balance, and my boyfriend's
homemade pizza.

RACHEL REIDER INTERIORS

20 Kirk St, West Roxbury, 617.942.2460
rachelreider.com

Fresh. Sophisticated. Unique.
Rachel Reider Interiors offers comprehensive design services for residential and commercial projects. Their work has been nationally recognized for its unique use of color, texture, and form to create a fresh and sophisticated take on timeless design. With each design project, the goal is to create a cohesive, well-balanced, and engaging space that reflects the unique personality of each individual client.

Main photo (this page) by Rare Brick, top left photo (opposite page) by Kat Rea Photography, top middle and right photos (opposite page) by Robert Orr Photography, portrait by Migan Ang

Rachel
Reider

 Q and A

What or who inspired you to start your business?
My passion for interior design. I feel so lucky
that I am able to apply my interests and
passions to my work. I truly love what I do!

How do you spend your free time?
Traveling! New places ignite my creativity;
you never know where you'll find inspiration.
It's also a great means to stay connected to
new and exciting products and sources.

What is your indulgence?
Home decor accessories. It's amazing
what a difference great accessories can
make in a space. The right pillow or vase
with a pop of color or pattern can instantly
change the look and feel of a room.

Who is your role model or mentor?
My parents. They each own their own
business, and provide amazing examples
of hard work, integrity, and creativity.

RHOOST

617.240.3948
rhoost.com, Twitter: @rhoosting

Functional. Stylish. Eco-friendly.
Safety, meet style. Rhoost provides parents with functional and stylish baby-proofing products. Rhoost Edge table corner protectors turn sharp edges into furniture fashion statements. Rhoost Slings are chic and simple and keep cute and curious hands out of off-limit cabinets. Rhoost is committed to using materials that are free of BPA, lead, and phthalate, and all products and packaging are 100 percent recyclable.

Tavinder Phull and Vianka Perez Belyea

Q and A

What are your most popular products or services?
Given that we are new to the market,
we are eager to find that out!

What or who inspired you to start your business?
Who: Soledad, Vianka's daughter. What:
wanting a product that did not exist.

Who is your role model or mentor?
Our own mothers and grandmothers.

What business mistake have you
made that you will not repeat?
Overprocessing decisions—go with your gut.

How do you spend your free time?
With friends and family—preferably while traveling!

What is your indulgence?
Dry white wine and stinky cheese.

Kathie and
Lindsey Fieldman

What are your most popular
products or services?
Our identité line of vintage-inspired
personalized jewelry. Everyone goes crazy
for the mama and love necklaces.

People may be surprised to know...
Like many moms and daughters, we
laugh, cry, and argue—but our trust in
each other trumps our differences.

What or who inspired you to
start your business?
The joy of creating and the
entrepreneurial spirit.

Where is your favorite place to
go with your girlfriends?
We love to explore Boston's neighborhoods.
We get inspired by discovering unique retail
venues, art districts, and flea markets.

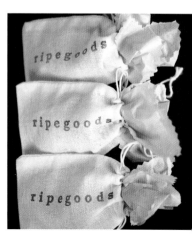

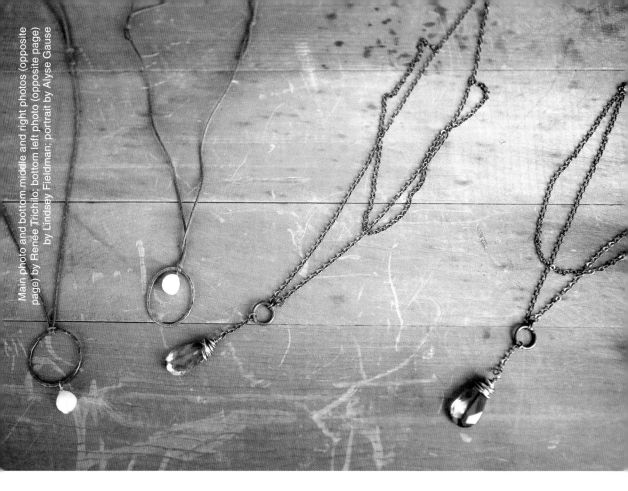

Main photo and bottom-middle and right photos (opposite page) by Renee Trichlo; bottom left photo (opposite page) by Lindsey Fieldman; portrait by Alyse Gause

RIPEGOODS

617.504.3393
ripegoods.com, Twitter: @ripegoods

Urban. Rustic. Simple.
Ripegoods founders, mother-and-daughter design team Kathie and Lindsey Fieldman, craft botanically inspired jewelry and note cards with an urban, rustic feel. Their mission is to create original designs for body and soul using local, eco-friendly materials. Find a gorgeous balance of earthy, simple, and delicate goods in their online boutique as well as at unique markets and trunk shows throughout the Boston area.

ROUGE COSMETICS

322 Derby St, Salem, 978.740.1044
rouge.com, Twitter: @rougecosmetics

Beautiful. Fun. Friendly.
Find out for yourself why Rouge has been voted the best place to get makeup, skincare, and expert advice. At Rouge, you are encouraged to explore the great selection of makeup, skin care and fragrances, including Stila, NARS, bareMinerals, Paula Dorf, glominerals, Darphin, Caudalie, Mario Badescu, Bumble and bumble, Tocca, Ineke, Clarisonic, COOLA, Neil Morris, blinc, The Art of Shaving, and many more. Rouge also specializes in wedding and special event makeup application and lessons, and hosts girls' nights out and bachelorette parties!

Photos by Leigh Smyth of Oh Snap! photography

Ann Supple Massey

 $\mathcal{Q}$ and $\mathcal{A}$

What are your most popular products or services?
Bridal makeup application, bareMinerals, the
lip scrub, Caudalie skincare, and glominerals.

People may be surprised to know...
We do fabulous false-lash applications.
It's the most natural way to glam
up your eyes for an event!

How do you spend your free time?
Reading, skiing, running, carpooling, and
watching my kids' baseball and softball games.

Where is your favorite place to
go with your girlfriends?
Out to dinner for delicious food and wine,
preferably in restaurants with female chefs!

What do you CRAVE? In business? In life?
Success, balance, health, fun, and peace!

What do you CRAVE?
In business? In life?

"*Enough income to live the way I want and enough free time to live it!*"

Leise Jones of Leise Jones Photography

Jennifer Saphier

Q and A

What are your most popular products or services?
Start-to-finish event planning for everything from fund-raisers and weddings to galas and grand openings. We also have a huge stash of one-of-a-kind decor items.

People may be surprised to know...
We handle more than just logistics. We can help with decor design, staffing, and even connecting you with sponsors and vendors for your event.

Where is your favorite place to go with your girlfriends?
We host the most fabulous swap parties. They are a total blast!

What do you CRAVE? In business? In life?
The ability to combine everything I love and am passionate about into aspects of my everyday life.

SAPHIER EVENTS

617.416.0013
saphierevents.com, Twitter: @saphierevents

Personal. Creative. Effective.
Saphier Events' inventive decor ideas and out-of-the-box solutions set them apart. Paying attention to their clients' needs down to the smallest detail, they ensure that the planning process is almost as fun as the event itself. They creatively brand promotional events, stunning weddings, and memorable fund-raisers. Saphier Events is a one-stop event-planning shop.

Photos by Janel Robertson, except main photo (this page), by Jennifer Saphier

SARRA

840 Summer St, Boston, 617.269.8999
104A North St, Hingham, 781.749.5599
sarrastudios.com

Informative. Fresh. Inviting.
Sarra offers a unique alternative to the makeup counter experience. Their talented personal image stylists provide clients with luxurious products and services, including precision brow shaping, makeup application, and makeup lessons that are unparalleled. With a focus on natural beauty and education, they successfully take the mystery out of a woman's search to look her best every day.

Photos by Renee Trichilo

Lauren Genatossio

Q and A

What are your most popular products or services?
Our 30-minute precision brow shaping which
uses only tweezers, scissors, and a few secret
tricks to uncover your true brow shape. It is truly
a miracle. Also, our two-hour makeup lesson.
We go through your makeup bag with you,
assessing your individual needs and teaching
you how to execute the perfect look. Our private
label skin care and makeup line will help you
recreate your new look at home with ease.

People may be surprised to know...
I became a makeup artist by accident,
and I was lucky to have stumbled upon
this path. My studios are named after my
grandmother, Sarra (pronounced sa-ray).
She was a makeup artist, so she must have
had something to do with this twist of fate.

Photos by Nina Gallant

SCRIBE PAPER & GIFT

84 Washington St, Marblehead, 781.631.7274
scribepaper.com, Twitter: @scribepapergift

Colorful. Fresh. Fun.
Scribe Paper & Gift is overflowing with unique gifts for every occasion and an amazing selection of greeting cards. Plan to spend some time exploring this North Shore boutique, since there is much to discover. Elegant wedding invitations feature some of the finest letterpress printers in the industry. The great mix of merchandise has ranked Scribe Paper & Gift "Best of Boston" and "Best of the New" in *Boston Globe Magazine*.

Q and A

Grace Cole

What are your most popular products or services?
Everything can be personalized: stationery monogrammed while you wait; frames, buckets, and more marked with your personal stamp!

What or who inspired you to start your business?
My love of great cards—the workmanship of the handmade cards and the quippy maxim one-liners that capture just the right sentiment for the occasion!

What business mistake have you made that you will not repeat?
Allowing personal feelings to influence business decisions. Whether it's hiring help or buying merchandise, you have to leave the personal stuff behind to make good business decisions.

What is your indulgence?
I am a paper snob, so, of course, I have *beautiful* stationery!

Courtney Heath

Q and A

What are your most popular products or services?
It's not necessarily a product or a service, but more a philosophy at Seed Stitch: People are attracted to the atmosphere, the comfort, and sense of community they feel when they walk in. When they have a challenge with a project or in their life, customers are welcome to come in, sit down, and work at any time.

What or who inspired you to start your business?
The desire to make a difference in the community and be my own boss. Owning a business was a perfect answer.

What is your indulgence?
Chocolate. Plain and simple.

What do you CRAVE? In business? In life?
Creativity, inspiration, laughter, and contentment.

SEED STITCH FINE YARN

21 Front St, Salem, 978.744.5557
seedstitchfineyarn.com, Twitter: @seedstitch

Creative. Inspirational. Welcoming.
Knitters, crocheters, and fiber artists from far and wide seek out Seed Stitch Fine Yarn for a wide array of yarns, patterns, accessories, classes, inspiration, and more. Specializing in natural fibers from luxury cashmere to workhorse wools, Seed Stitch has it all. The store's helpful and welcoming staff can assist you whether you're working on your 500th project or your first. At Seed Stitch, you'll find everyday inspiration ... every day!

Photos by Nina Gallant

SHE

86 Washington St, Marblehead, 781.639.9800
shemarblehead.com, Twitter: @shemarblehead

Compulsive. Diverse. Real.
She is a gem of a boutique located in historic downtown Marblehead. Offering a mix of contemporary clothing, the boutique is a place where both moms and daughters can enjoy a laid-back shopping experience. Dresses and tops are graceful and current. Premium denim and fashion tees satisfy that "just need something new" urge. Sales associates always encourage shoppers to keep their personal style while evolving their look.

Q and A

People may be surprised to know...
The store is in a pre-Civil War building. It used to be a hardware store. It's definitely haunted.

What or who inspired you to start your business?
I needed a change, and the opportunity presented itself. It was that simple and that complicated. I avoided advice that was discouraging.

Who is your role model or mentor?
My grandmother is very level-headed and low-key, and she doesn't judge. That is hard to achieve. She also plays a lot of poker and forwards me dirty jokes.

How do you spend your free time?
Taking my kids on adventures, reading and writing short stories, and catching up with long-distance friends.

What is your indulgence?
Me&Ro jewelry. It speaks my language!

Tiffany Gaddis

195

Fiona Gerety

 Q and A

What are your most popular
products or services?
Complimentary spa services, product-
stuffed swag bags, and one-of-a-
kind fashion pieces you simply can't
find in a traditional retail setting.

People may be surprised to know...
StyleFixx is going national! We've
successfully debuted in New York and are
now making our way down the coast.

Who is your role model or mentor?
I've always been inspired by the savvy
female entrepreneurs I encounter
every day through StyleFixx.

How do you spend your free time?
Curled up in bed in my pajamas
with a good book.

STYLEFIXX

617.719.9999
stylefixx.com, Twitter: @stylefixxevents

Stylish. Sophisticated. Interactive.
StyleFixx is Boston's premier shopping and nightlife event. Twice a year, thousands of style-conscious women gather for two nights of indulgence and dream shopping. Featuring more than 55 cutting-edge designers and brands, StyleFixx showcases exclusive services, emerging trends, and must-have products. Providing a true "evening out" experience, sophisticated women are pampered with complimentary spa services, cocktails, appetizers, music, and product-stuffed swag bags.

Photos by Fiona Gerety, except portrait by Leise Jones

TOPAZ

11 Dunster St, Cambridge, 617.492.3700
topazcambridge.com

Serene. Classy. Cutting-edge.
Topaz is the perfect little spot for anyone who needs something uniquely fabulous!
They feature jewelry and accessories designed to bring you compliments—sterling
silver, semi-precious stones, vintage style, handbags, and shawls—beautiful designs
from all around the world, and a great range of pricing. They spin great tunes, and their
creative staff will ensure your needs are met. You'll always find that perfect gift!

PASHMINA!
30% Silk - 70% Cashmere   .85-

Photos by Leise Jones

VETIVER
EAU DE PARFUM

Lavender
EAU DE PARFUM

Stephanie Dunn and Evelyn Levy

 Q and A

People may be surprised to know...
We have something in every price
range—$10 to $1,000.

What or who inspired you to start your business?
Our friendship, combined with a love of jewelry.

Who is your role model or mentor?
Any woman who has made it on her own,
starting at the bottom, and, against all odds,
has reached the top of her game, such as
Barbara Walters, Martha Stewart, and Oprah.

How do you spend your free time?
We practice yoga and meditation, go
on nature hikes, travel, and cook.

Where is your favorite place to
go with your girlfriends?
New York in the spring to shop, explore
trade shows, and attend concerts
at Radio City Music Hall.

What or who inspired you to
start your business?
My grandmother. She hated shopping,
so as a child, she'd take me to the store
and let me pick out her clothes!

People may be surprised to know...
I am addicted to Mountain Dew!

Who is your role model or mentor?
Rachel Zoe, a stylist who is dedicated
and has a great eye for fashion,
but remains true to herself.

How do you spend your free time?
With my puppy, watching him learn
and change as he grows.

Where is your favorite place to
go with your girlfriends?
We love to travel, and Las Vegas has
become quite a favorite lately!

Tricia
Cromwell

TRUST IN TRICIA

508.649.3296
itrustintricia.com

Creative. Stylish. Reliable.
Trust in Tricia offers personal shopping and wardrobe-consulting services. They analyze and evaluate men's and women's wardrobes to help them take the guessing out of dressing, as well as handle all of their shopping needs.

TURTLE

619A Tremont St, Boston, 617.266.2610
turtleboston.com

Stylish. Urban. Modern.
Turtle is a one-of-a-kind boutique in Boston's South End devoted to selling artisan and handmade women's clothing, jewelry, and accessories from emerging fashion designers and artists. Turtle offers products that are wearable, that challenge convention, and that enable people to express themselves both within and beyond established fashion trends.

Photos by Melissa Ostrow

Ann Dingwell

Q and A

What are your most popular products or services?
Although we carry several designers,
our most popular lines are Elm, Prairie
Underground, and Feral Childe.

People may be surprised to know...
The Turtle name and logo symbolize
"coming out of one's shell."

What or who inspired you to start your business?
I have worked in the Back Bay of Boston in high-
end boutiques for the past 20 years. It has always
been my dream to have my own boutique. Turtle
was being sold, and I jumped at the opportunity.

Who is your role model or mentor?
Grace Kelly with her charm and sophistication.

Where is your favorite place to
go with your girlfriends?
Getting a pedicure and eating sushi.

What or who inspired you to start your business?

" *The prospect of having to answer to myself alone for creative success or shortcoming was both scary and irresistible.* "

Andrea Morton of aMortonDesign

TWINKLE STAR BABY

7 Upland Road, Cambridge, 617.300.0177
shoptwinklestar.com, Twitter: @shoptwinklestar

Modern. Mindful. Adorable.
Twinkle Star is a baby and child boutique specializing in quality clothing, gear, and accessories.
This mom-and-pop boutique is locally owned by parents of young children. Each product is
scrutinized by them to assure its function and value. Since opening its doors in 2008, Twinkle
Star is the place for everything from pacifiers to exclusive European clothing imports.

Kerri Friedlaender

Q and A

What are your most popular products or services?
Swaddle blankets, mobiles, shoes, strollers,
Petunia Pickle Bottom diaper bags, and Kicky
Pants, our favorite bamboo clothing line.

People may be surprised to know...
We have an in-house photography studio called
"Twice As Nice Photography," specializing
in baby, child, and family portraits.

Who is your role model or mentor?
My husband and business partner, Lucas.
I admire his ability to work hard, but
also put business worries aside to enjoy
time with our family and friends.

What business mistake have you
made that you will not repeat?
Bringing in lower quality items in a
(failed) effort to increase sales when the
economic downturn hit full force.

TWO GIRLS SHOP

83 Washington St, Salem, 978.744.5191

Eclectic. Inspiring. Welcoming.
Two girls shop is an eclectic store new to the North Shore. From unusual reused and vintage home decor, to comfy jeans, T-shirts, and Bohemian jewelry, you will be pleasantly surprised by the fun assortment. One may find unique decor pieces next to contemporary funky kitchen items. Two girls shop offers an ever-changing array of treasures for you and your home.

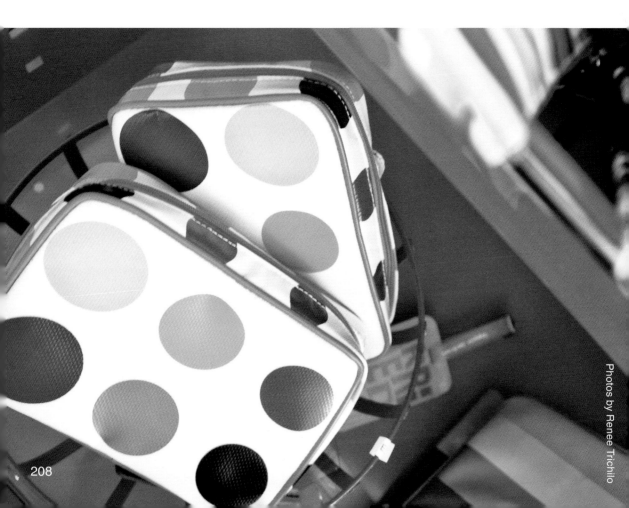

Photos by Renee Trichilo

Pia Schoeck and Emily Edelman

 $\mathcal{Q}$ and $\mathcal{A}$

What are your most popular products or services?
Vibrantly colored Tubtrugs, hot pink snail watering cans, *Porn for Women* books, recycled overnight totes, and kitchen whimsies.

What or who inspired you to start your business?
Our love for resourceful design and our respect for each other's creativity.

What business mistake have you made that you will not repeat?
Not realizing from the get-go that everyone does not share our positive outlook and that healthy competition is not something to be threatened by, but rather embraced and used as a source of growth.

What is your indulgence?
A moment alone, chocolate, and Prosecco.

Mary-Catherine Deibel and
Deborah Hughes (not pictured)

Q and A

What are your most popular
products or services?
We are open for all services, but
Saturday afternoon tea is a favorite,
as is the late-night bar menu.

People may be surprised to know...
Deborah designed the restaurant!

How do you spend your free time?
Reading; playing tournament croquet
with my champion husband, Reid
Fleming; and bike-riding.

What is your indulgence?
Having one of our signature
praline milk-chocolate turtles—an
indulgence worth the calories.

UPSTAIRS ON THE SQUARE

91 Winthrop St, Cambridge, 617.864.1933
upstairsonthesquare.com

Artisanal. Delicious. Fun.
Mary-Catherine Deibel and Deborah Hughes' restaurant, UpStairs on the Square, opened to great fanfare and glowing reviews. Named one of the 10 top new restaurants in the world by *Food & Wine*, it is now an institution in the heart of Harvard Square, with its two quirky, yet beautiful, fire-lit dining rooms—one casual, one pink and gold—and an exquisite menu.

Photos by Leise Jones

Q and A

What or who inspired you to start your business?
I started reading books about living in the moment, changing my way of thinking, and began to meditate and visualize what I truly wanted. I was actually meditating and saw Urban Elements in my mind. The feeling was so powerful!

Who is your role model or mentor?
My mom. She has always taught me the importance of honesty, strength, courage, and believing in myself.

What do you CRAVE? In business? In life?
Always challenging myself to grow, to be positive, to love and live in the now, to inspire people, and to make the world better by living life in this way.

Kim
Tenenbaum

URBAN ELEMENTS HOME & GIFTS

230 Essex St, Salem, 978.666.4408
urbanelementshome.com, Twitter: @urban_elements

Hip. Chic. Stylish.
Urban Elements offers a blend of unique home goods, one-of-a-kind furniture, candles, handbags and wallets, belts, bracelets and jewelry, and much more. Owner Kim Tenenbaum aspires to become a life coach, so many of the items have positive meaning. You feel the good energy as soon as you walk in the door!

THE URBAN HOUND HOTEL

129 Malden St, Boston, 617.755.5775
urbanhounds.com, Twitter: @theurbanhound

Modern. Innovative. Luxurious.
A simple formula: care + luxury + innovation = a happy dog. The Urban Hound Hotel is Boston's first luxury day care and overnight facility featuring 8,500 square feet of the latest in animal-care innovations and technologies. Their state-of-the-art facility parallels a dog's natural instincts, ensuring the highest level of health and safety for dogs of all shapes and sizes.

Main photo (this page) and portrait by Renee Trichilo, top left and right photos (opposite page) by Jessica Barker Photography, top middle photo (opposite page) by Kim Grisco Photography

Rebecca Willson

Q and A

What are your most popular products or services?
Our most popular services are our customized puppy programs, off-leash day hikes, day care, and boarding.

What or who inspired you to start your business?
My wife, Michelle, inspired me to start The Urban Hound. After years of her listening to my desire to work with dogs, she gave me the push I needed to believe in myself, start my own business, and do what I have always wanted to do—work with dogs every day!

Where is your favorite place to go with your girlfriends?
The Farmers Market at Copley for cooking inspiration, my roof deck to relax, and out to dinner at Oleana for a fantastic dinner on their patio.

THE VELVET FLY

28 Parmenter St, Boston, 617.557.4359
thevelvetfly.com, Twitter: @velvetflygirl

Feminine. Eclectic. Playful.
The Velvet Fly prevails as the North End's most feminine boutique with a crafty-cool aesthetic that boasts a small hand-selected collection of vintage classics alongside new retro-inspired designers. The juxtaposition of old and new is tailored for women with discerning taste who are looking to add personality to their existing wardrobe using modern and one-of-a-kind vintage pieces.

BethAnn Hoyos and Lorrinda Cerrutti

Q and A

What are your most popular products or services?
Our dresses, whether vintage or from
our contemporary designers, keep our
customers coming back time and again.

People may be surprised to know...
We actually *hate* dressing ourselves,
but *love* dressing other people!

Who is your role model or mentor?
Ellen DeGeneres, because she takes risks,
is extremely generous, and loves life.

How do you spend your free time?
When we're not at the store, we are playing
at the park, chasing after our kids.

What do you CRAVE? In business? In life?
Balance between work and play is what
we strive for in all aspects of our lives.

Valerie Conyngham

 Q and A

What are your most popular
products or services?
People love my in-home chocolate parties—a
delicious way to spend time with friends
while making and eating lots of chocolate.

What or who inspired you to
start your business?
A collection of encouraging words
from friends and family.

How do you spend your free time?
Exploring all the city has to offer.

Where is your favorite place to
go with your girlfriends?
At each others' homes, gossiping
over a good bottle of wine.

What do you CRAVE? In business? In life?
Understanding, happiness, and success
for myself and the people around me.

VIANNE CHOCOLAT

617.901.1624
viannechocolat.com, Twitter: @viannechocolat

Indulgent. Flavorful. Luxurious.
Vianne chocolat makes handmade artisan chocolates with a touch of local flavor. Starting with a blend of the world's best couvertures, they add fresh cream and butter from New England dairies, and wonderful flavor infusions of herbs, spices, liqueurs, fruits, and more. Vianne chocolat is perfect for self-indulgence, wedding favors, as well as corporate gifts.

Lisa
Cancelli

Q and A

What are your most popular products or services?
Viola Lovely definitely has its accessory devotees! Over time, this has evolved into personal styling and consulting for clients and vendors.

People may be surprised to know...
The store was named after my nana, Viola Picard, and the "Lovely" was added two years later, since it best defined the women that have supported and inspired my vision.

What business mistake have you made that you will not repeat?
Not knowing that it's "okay" to say no, and that you can't be all things to all people. Know your strengths, and what you do best, and stay the course.

Where is your favorite place to go with your girlfriends?
The back room of viola Lovely when new product arrives.

VIOLA LOVELY

15 Walnut Road, South Hamilton, 978.468.1775
148 Main St, Wenham, 978.468.1775
38 Main St, Concord, 978.287.0775
violalovely.com, Twitter: @violalovely

Smart. Beautiful. Intriguing.
Viola Lovely is an award-winning lifestyle boutique with an ever-evolving selection of shoes, apparel, and accessories. Offering directional, yet approachable style in a lounge-like atmosphere, viola Lovely hand-selects product from the latest designers, often being one of the first to discover new talent, such as Loeffler Randall, Leigh & Luca, and Gemma Redux.

THE WINE BOTTEGA

341 Hanover St, Boston, 617.227.6607
thewinebottega.com, Twitter: @kerplatt11

Unexpected. Intelligent. Adventurous.
The Wine Bottega seeks out and sells wines from the coolest, craziest, happiest wine-makers on the planet. They specialize in natural, wines that allow the personality of the grapes, region, and growing season to shine through. Every wine has a unique story to tell and offers the chance to travel the globe in one sip.

Photos by Leise Jones

Kerri Platt

 Q and A

What are your most popular products or services?
The staff! Vintages will come and go,
favorites change daily, but it's knowledge and
passion that keep people coming back.

Who is your role model or mentor?
Julia Child. She wasn't afraid to be
herself and was so full of life!

What is your indulgence?
Dining out. Great food and wine are my spa
treatment and retail therapy combined.

Where is your favorite place to
go with your girlfriends?
Chinatown! I moved there a year ago and
am still discovering amazing places.

What do you CRAVE? In business? In life?
Change, friendship, sincerity, bringing a
little slice of happiness to others whenever
I can, and more wine, of course!

Stephanie Willson and Jane Rudnick

 Q and A

What are your most popular products or services?
Popular producst include flirty dresses, cozy cashmere, trendy Chan Luu wrap bracelets, perfectly fitting denim, and Luxe leather handbags. Customers also love our events, such as girls' nights, trunk shows, and private parties.

Where is your favorite place to go with your girlfriends?
Bella Sante Spa on Newbury Street, followed by dinner and cocktails.

What do you CRAVE? In business? In life?
Success, both personally and in business, through peace, honesty, and feeling beautiful.

What is your indulgence?
Fabulous shoes!

WISH

49 Charles St, Boston, 617.227.4441
wishboston.com

Fun. Stylish. Feminine.
Wish is a specialty boutique located in the heart of charming and historic Beacon Hill. For
10 years they have provided women with a fun and unique shopping experience. They pride
themselves on finding the very best from favorite designers, such as Milly, Diane von Fürstenberg,
Trina Turk, Tibi, Rebecca Taylor, Susana Monaco, Ella Moss, Hudson, and many more.

Photos by Leigh Smyth of Oh Snap! photography

Intelligentsia Directory

Business-to-business entreprenesses, including coaching, marketing and public relations, photography, business consulting, and design services.

1-STOP DESIGN SHOP, INC.

25 Hart Place, Woburn, 781.938.3866
1stopdesign.com, 1stopteam.wordpress.com, Twitter: @1StopDesignShop

Creative. Effective. Proven.
1-Stop Design Shop helps partners distinguish their brand, grow market share, and increase revenue through integrated service and social media solutions. They leverage proven people, processes, and technologies to build businesses. From concepts to copy writing, photography, and corporate brand design to website creation, hosting, multimedia, email marketing, and metric analytics, 1-Stop produces measurable business results for their clients.

Photo by Chris Hennigan

Christine Hennigan

 Q and A

People may be surprised to know...
How relaxed the 1-Stop is. We work in such a close, creative environment, it's easy for us to become more than just coworkers. We depend on each other for balance, honesty, criticism, and to keep each other laughing. Without laughter the creative juices tend to get a bit dry.

Who is your role model or mentor?
My Aunt Ann is the reason I'm a graphic designer. I followed in her footsteps by going to the same art school, Montserrat College of Art. As a young girl I would watch her paint and dream of doing what she did. She still works in the field down on Cape Cod and is also an entrepreneur.

What do you CRAVE? In business? In life?
Serenity and peace ... a few minutes of quiet in my life when I can stop and focus on the moment.

ABCLARKE COACHING

857.244.1853
setting-and-achieving-goals.com, Twitter: @abclarke

Dynamic. Personal. Connected.
Anne Clarke of ABClarke Coaching is an executive, personal coach, and motivational speaker. She is passionate about helping others achieve success, however they define it, with a bit of old-fashioned *la dolce vita* (the good life) thrown in. With attentive listening, deliberate focus, gentle encouragement, humor, and insight, Anne helps her many clients make lasting, manageable, satisfying, positive changes.

Anne Clarke

Q and A

What or who inspired you to start your business?
A good friend asked, "Have you heard of coaching? I think you would be great at it." And it was one of those life-changing moments. I had found my calling.

What business mistake have you made that you will not repeat?
My early days on the Internet with a poorly designed, rarely visited site are a mistake I will not repeat again.

How do you spend your free time?
Cooking, reading, traveling, going to the movies, and being outside.

Where is your favorite place to go with your girlfriends?
Dinner and a show on Broadway in New York City.

AMORTONDESIGN

25 Prescott St, Somerville, 617.894.0285
aMortonDesign.com

Sustainable. Adaptable. Personal.
Architecture firm aMortonDesign provides innovative contextual solutions with a focus on sustainable design and green consulting to LEED and beyond. Whether in a home, work space, learning environment, or cultural institution, the common denominator is people. Architecture should meet human needs, provide inspiration, and enhance lives, experiences, and surroundings.

Photo by Erin Wells Design

Andrea Morton

What are your most popular products or services?
Kitchen and bathroom renovations are popular ways to add personal flair to homes and increase energy efficiency.

People may be surprised to know...
I have a theater background, which informs my approach to color, lighting, and spatial organization.

What is your indulgence?
Travel is my guilty pleasure because it expands my carbon footprint but opens my mind like nothing else.

Where is your favorite place to go with your girlfriends?
Christina's Ice Cream in Cambridge for delicious, unique, and seasonal fresh flavors.

BERLUTI & MCLAUGHLIN LLC

44 School St, 9th Floor, Boston, 617.557.3030
bermac-law.com

Efficient. Effective. Nimble.
Berluti & McLaughlin is a law firm that serves as general counsel to entrepreneurs
and small- to mid-size businesses (including tech start-ups, retail establishments,
and service providers). Taking time to learn about clients, they offer targeted advice
to best suit your goals. Cost-conscious and effective, Berluti & McLaughlin have the
experience to meet both straightforward and sophisticated legal challenges.

Kimberly Kramer

Q and A

What are your most popular
products or services?
Forming new entities and helping clients
negotiate business contracts and the
terms of partnerships or joint ventures.

People may be surprised to know...
I commute by bike from Somerville. It
helps me transition from home to work
and back, and I get some fresh air!

Who is your role model or mentor?
My partner, John McLaughlin, who
is an amazing mentor and friend,
and my mother, who is somehow
always right about everything.

What business mistake have you
made that you will not repeat?
Believing the misconception that real
work is always done behind a desk.

Photo by Ed MacKinnon Photography

IN FULL FORCE

617.840.1965
infullforce.com, Twitter: @InFullForce

Dynamic. Persuasive. Exciting.
In Full Force works tirelessly to create passion and excitement for your brand. Whether you need a website, event, advertising, copy writing, or simply a brilliant idea, they love tackling challenges, creating innovative solutions, and producing amazing results. In Full Force is poised to react quickly and intelligently to make sense of your marketplace and cleverly communicate your brand.

Julie O'Brien Fairweather

Photo by Helene Norton Russell

 Q and A

What are your most popular
products or services?
Events are our most popular product. They are successful thanks to our most popular service: our creative and ingenious marketing skills.

People may be surprised to know...
Moving consumers via smart marketing doesn't have to cost a fortune.

Who is your role model or mentor?
My role model is myself. I strive to become everything I believe I can be, because who I think I can become is pretty amazing.

What business mistake have you made that you will not repeat?
Trying to grow too quickly. Slow and steady wins the race.

JESSICA SUTTON GRAPHIC DESIGN

369 Congress St, 2nd Floor, Boston, 603.548.6760
jessicasutton.com, Twitter: @jsgraphicdesign

Passionate. Refined. Innovative.

From fashion blogistas to urban dog walkers, Jessica Sutton Graphic Design leads clients into the exciting world of logo and collateral development, website creation, and social networking perfection. They design company identities for businesses large and small, helping them establish a strong brand and aesthetic.

Photo by Sarah Winchester Studios

Jessica Sutton

Q and A

What or who inspired you to start your business?
I took the leap into being a business owner when I could no longer balance my freelance design with my full-time job.

Who is your role model or mentor?
Alina Roytberg, co-founder of Fresh, has both influenced my design aesthetic and shown me what it takes to be a strong female entrepreneur.

Where is your favorite place to go with your girlfriends?
Drink and Sportello, since both are across from the studio and delicious. I also love Deluxe in the South End.

What do you CRAVE? In business? In life?
In business, good clients and beautiful design. In life, endless yoga/surf retreats and sunshine.

KIRSTEN AMANN
FREELANCE WRITING + PUBLIC RELATIONS

617.733.2791
kirstenamann.com, Twitter: @kirstenamann

Creative. Innovative. Vibrant.
Kirsten Amann is an independent lifestyle publicist, freelance writer, and founding member of the Boston chapter of Ladies United for the Preservation of Endangered Cocktails. Kirsten crafts public relations campaigns for a variety of lifestyle clients both locally and nationally, with niche expertise in spirits, wine, and food. She writes about cocktails for *The Weekly Dig* and *Massachusetts Beverage Business*, among others.

Photo by Matt Demers

Kirsten Amann

Q and A

What are your most popular products or services?
Media relations, message planning, positioning, event planning and execution, and cocktail development.

People may be surprised to know...
I was born in New Jersey and used to have a very thick Jersey-girl accent!

What or who inspired you to start your business?
The perfect job for me didn't seem to exist, so I decided to make it up myself.

How do you spend your free time?
Practicing yoga, learning French and Italian, studying wine, experimenting with cocktails, cooking, and baking.

LEISE JONES PHOTOGRAPHY

617.671.5572
leisejones.com

Natural. Creative. Smart.

Leise Jones is a documentary and lifestyle photographer who works throughout New England with families, small businesses, restaurants, and non-profit groups. Her work reflects her lifestyle—simple, progressive, and straightforward. As a result, her photographs are always honest and natural-looking, never over-produced or flashy. Leise's goal is to make pictures that have meaning, both for her and her clients.

Leise Jones

Q and A

What or who inspired you to start your business?
I became a full-time freelancer so that I could control my schedule and work on the projects that I am most passionate about. As a photographer, every day is different. It keeps me on my toes.

What business mistake have you made that you will not repeat?
Doing too much for free. In the beginning, I didn't value my work enough to actually charge decent rates for it. I had to learn that my services were valuable.

Where is your favorite place to go with your girlfriends?
Cuchi-Cuchi in Cambridge is my favorite place for fun cocktails and flirty bartenders.

MARQUIS DESIGN

9 Hamilton Pl, Ste 300, Boston, 617.426.1470
marquisdesign.com, Twitter: @marquisdesign

Strategic. Creative. Trustworthy.
Marquis Design is an award-winning strategic branding and graphic design firm specializing in hospitality, events, luxury, lifestyle, and business-to-business. They sync every facet of your brand personality—your voice, image, and distinct position in your industry—to create stronger and deeper customer relationships. Everything from print to web is sure to make customers say, "wow."

Julie Vail

 Q and A

What are your most popular products or services?
Helping organizations create their own unique brand personality. We uncover and capture your true essence and communicate these values through integrated marketing campaigns.

People may be surprised to know...
A girl who grew up in a New York Yankees family was hired by the Boston Red Sox to create their brand for their Fenway Park events business.

What do you CRAVE? In business? In life?
Seeing a client's eyes light up when we present our work to them. Nothing brings me greater joy than exceeding our clients' expectations.

MELOPHOTO

516.455.0463
melophoto.net

Dynamic. Creative. Captivating.
As a photojournalist, every day is something different for Melissa Ostrow. A dynamic photographer, she shoots everything from events, conferences, and interiors, to product shots, food, and portraits. Her work experience includes a myriad of publications and websites, PR companies, non-profits, and major corporations, such as Absolut, Puma, Pepsi, Adidas, and many more.

Photo by Melissa Ostrow

Melissa Ostrow

Q and A

What are your most popular
products or services?
Shooting events, food, portraits, and
interior architectural photography.

Who is your role model or mentor?
My mother. I know it's a cliché. She
always tries to put forth her best, and
has taught me to do the same.

How do you spend your free time?
Exploring. There is always something
new to see or do, you just have
to go out there and find it.

Where is your favorite place to
go with your girlfriends?
Good Life to enjoy a cocktail
and some dancing.

PENNY SCHULER
BRAND IMAGING

781.962.8622
pennyschuler.com

Fresh. Smart. Creative.
Penny Schuler Brand Imaging develops brand identity using brand positioning; logo design; marketing; advertising; media planning and execution; website design; and print, radio, and television campaigns—whatever it takes to reach the objective.

Photo by Renee Trichilo

Penny Schuler

 Q and A

What or who inspired you to start your business?
Necessity, the mother of invention.

What are your most popular products or services?
Logo and website design.

People may be surprised to know...
I have a secret garden.

What business mistake have you made that you will not repeat?
Underestimating how long a project will take. Not sure I won't make this one again, but it's a goal.

What do you CRAVE? In business? In life?
In business, doing great work for great clients. In life, health, happy children, and my husband till I take my last breath.

PHI DESIGN GROUP

617.838.3062

phidesigngroup.com, translateyourcreativedna.blogspot.com, Twitter: @phidesigngroup

Innovative. Bold. Personal.

PHI DESIGN GROUP is a full-service design consulting firm dedicated to creating transformative solutions for clients' needs and business goals. Using their distinct and immeasurable resources, they innovate a creative vision in all areas of design: commercial and residential interior design and space planning, event design and production, business development and marketing, personal styling, and coaching.

Photo by Renee Trichilo

Michelle Gubitosa and Nilda Martin

Q and A

What or who inspired you to start your business?
A deep desire to connect and make accessible design for all disciplines. Even in a traditional business environment, design is essential to success.

What is your indulgence?
Shoes, jewelry, watches, BeDazzlers, power tools, cameras, chocolate, Champagne, and always, time with friends and loved ones.

Where is your favorite place to go with your girlfriends?
Starlight Lounge (Michelle's roof deck), Bristol Lounge, and any lounge or beach with a cocktail.

What business mistake have you made that you will not repeat?
Not getting a deposit or signed contract. Never again!

PINKERGREEN

46 Waltham St, Ste 308, Boston, 617.532.1081
pinkergreen.com, Twitter: @pinkergreen

Creative. Intuitive. Passionate.

Pinkergreen is an award-winning branding and design firm specializing in robust campaigns consisting of identity development, print collateral, and web design. Since 2002, they set out to be eco-friendly in production, social in networking, and aware of new ventures. With progressive talents and a diligent mission-minded focus, Pinkergreen provides a range of businesses with creative solutions for their changing needs.

Kelley
Shaw-Wade

Photo by Lindsay Shaw Photography

Q and A

What are your most popular products or services?
Branding—encompassing everything from logo design to website development and every detail in-between.

What or who inspired you to start your business?
I visited a few South End graphic design studios in 2002. Their beautiful work and passion for their clients inspired the launch of Pinkergreen.

Where is your favorite place to go with your girlfriends?
Shamefully, we love karaoke, and usually head to either Limelight or DoReMi, followed by cocktails and Japanese hot-pot at Kaze Shabu Shabu in Chinatown.

R&L ASSOCIATES, INC.

100 Cummings Center, Ste 219Q, Beverly, 978.524.7750
rlassociatesinc.net, Twitter: @RLAssociatesInc

THE ARIES GROUP

100 Cummings Center, Ste 219Q, Beverly, 978.524.7750
ariesgroupinc.com, Twitter: @AriesGroupInc

Experienced. Excellent. Exceptional.
R&L is an award-winning, full-service, temp-to-hire and permanent placement agency specializing in administrative, accounting/banking, customer service, engineering, and light industrial staffing. For more than 35 years, R&L has provided experience, excellence, and exceptional services to their candidates and clients.

Q and A

Photo by Nancy D'Anna

Fran Dichner

People may be surprised to know...
R&L is a women owned, WBENC certified agency recognized as one of the top 10 recruiting firms in Massachusetts.

Who is your role model or mentor?
Linda Rappaport of Gazelle Strategic Partners.

What business mistake have you made that you will not repeat?
Unclear professional boundaries— becoming too personally involved with my staff and treating the relationship too much as a friendship.

What do you CRAVE? In business? In life?
Building my business to a level where I can continue to have the resources to remain philanthropic and mentor young women in business. Living a purpose-driven life.

RENEE TRICHILO
PHOTOGRAPHY

7 Upland Road, Cambridge, 617.285.3241
reneetrichilo.com

Fun. Simple. Vibrant.
Whether in-studio, on-location, or in your home, photographer Renee Trichilo creates beautiful images that capture your life, allow your child's unique spirit to shine through, and showcase your family's love. Renee specializes in portrait, wedding, and event photography. Her style is fun, classic, journalistic, emotional, ethereal, and airy.

Photo by Renee Trichilo

Renee Trichilo

Q and A

People may be surprised to know...
I co-own of TwiceAsNice Photography with my business partner Allison LeBlanc.

How do you spend your free time?
With the three most important people in my life: my husband, Sandro and our two boys, Alexio and Alessandro.

Who is your role model or mentor?
My husband. His continued support and motivation keeps me striving for the best in all that I do.

Where is your favorite place to go with your girlfriends?
Bisuteki. There is nothing like great company and great food!

SAVAS STUDIOS

617.728.7775
savasstudios.com

Captivating. Ardent. Unique.
Savas Studios is the dynamic sister team of Christine Savas, a makeup artist, and Stephanie Savas, a photographer. Christine received her certification in makeup artistry at the Lia Schorr Institute in New York, while Stephanie received a degree in photojournalism from Boston University. Producing photoshoots has always been a passion of theirs, and Savas Studios is the realization of that dream.

Photo by Savas Studios

Stephanie and Christine Savas

Q and A

What are your most popular products or services?
Our most popular services are portraits and pin-up photo shoots.

What or who inspired you to start your business?
Our passion for art and photography. Our business allows us to do what we love.

What business mistake have you made that you will not repeat?
Working on projects for little or no monetary compensation.

Who is your role model or mentor?
Our mother. She taught us to be passionate about what we love, and to follow our hearts and dreams.

SCORE MORE SALES, MORE SALES FUNDRAISING

888.883.8370
scoremoresales.com, Twitter: @scoremoresales

Amazing. Strategic. Fabulous.

Lori Richardson is a sales detective. She works like *CSI Miami* to listen to how a business offers its products and services, then makes up to 20 recommendations, generating a 20–75 percent increase in revenues. She also works with non-profits to grow mighty causes. She's raised millions of dollars and helped others to do the same.

Photo by Tara Gimmer Photography

Lori Richardson

 Q and A

People may be surprised to know...
I am a fast-talking, fundraising auctioneer. I am traveling around the United States in 2010 and abroad in 2011, speaking with small business owners and non-profits.

Who is your role model or mentor?
My grandmother, Mimi—she owned a women's retail apparel store and I worked for her from the time I was eight years old.

What business mistake have you made that you will not repeat?
Working without a plan. You cannot regain the time you put out there, so maximize every hour of your business.

What do you CRAVE? In business? In life?
I love being around passionate, committed people. Live life to the fullest. Don't compromise your beliefs for short-term gains.

SURGE

781.484.6899

Quick. Resourceful. Dependable.
Owner Gina Field provides infrastructure solutions and services to small businesses that usually only large companies can afford to sustain permanently. Services include operations organization assistance, short-term project management, market research, topic research to support preparation for important encounters such as customer and regulatory meetings. Business support products include research (such as inventory management) and accounting software.

Gina Field

 Q and A

What are your most popular
products or services?
Devising options for improved organization
and function, special topic research for
business markets, states of technology,
controversial issues, and sensitive topics.

What or who inspired you to
start your business?
An acquaintance observed me in action
and noted my superior ability to research an
issue and organize information and action.

What is your indulgence?
Books, unusual plants, great cookware,
expensive candles, and fine clothing
that will be with me for a long time.

Where is your favorite place to
go with your girlfriends?
Lectures on social and environmental
issues and private and public gardens.

WOMEN ON THE MOVE LLC

781.631.7588
womenonthemovellc.com

Knowledgeable. Skillful. Cost-effective.
Women on the Move takes the trauma out of moving! Managing the packing and
moving needs for working families in large and small homes, apartments, and offices,
Women on the Move provides a level of service and care that developed during
the process of servicing customers under highly stressful, time-constricted, life-changing
circumstances around a household and/or business move.

Annmarie
Linnane

Q and A

**What or who inspired you to
start your business?**
My previous career was in market development
in the pharmaceutical world. I successfully
built niche markets and departments within
"corporate life," but always had a desire to build
my own business. I personally moved 12 times
worldwide and was aware of the significant
gaps in the executive moving industry. When
the opportunity was offered to take over
Women on the Move, I jumped at the idea.

**Where is your favorite place to
go with your girlfriends?**
Restaurants of well-known chefs,
spas, and picnics on the beach.

How do you spend your free time?
Sailing, skiing, reading, and sipping wine.

Contributors

At CRAVE Boston, we believe in acknowledging, celebrating, and passionately supporting locally owned businesses and entrepreneurs. We are extremely grateful to all of the contributors for this publication.

Amanda Buzard
lead designer and editor
amandabuzard.com

Amanda is a Seattle-based designer inspired by clean patterns and bold textiles. She chases many creative and active pursuits in her spare time. Passions include Northwest travel, photography, dining out, and creating community.

Nicole Shema
project manager
nicole@thecravecompany.com

Nicole graduated from the University of Oregon in June 2009 with bachelor's degrees in economics and political science, and then moved back to her hometown of Seattle. She has been with CRAVE since September 2009.

Lilla Kovacs
operations manager
lilla@thecravecompany.com

Lilla has been with CRAVE since 2005. As the operations manager, she ensures that everything runs like clockwork. She loves shoe shopping, traveling, art, and her MacBook.

Alison Turner
graphic designer
alisonjturner.com

Alison is a graphic designer, seamstress, and block printer from Seattle who supports human rights and the local food movement. In her spare time she enjoys music, cooking, and being outside.

Alison Peacock
copy editor
peacockweddings.com

Alison Peacock is a writer, editor, and photographer with 18 years of journalism experience. When she's not copyediting books about savvy businesswomen, she focuses her camera on her favorite subject: weddings.

Carrie Wicks
proofreader and copyeditor
linkedin.com/in/carriewicks

Carrie Wicks has been proofreading professionally for 14-plus years in mostly creative fields. When she's not proofreading or copyediting, she's reading, singing jazz, walking in the woods, or gardening.

Leise Jones
photographer
leisejones.com

Leise Jones is a freelance photographer based in Jamaica Plain. She is passionate about photographing food, special events, natural-looking portraits, and documenting the untold stories of our communities.

Melissa Ostrow
photographer
melophoto.net

A dynamic photographer, Melissa Ostrow captures everything from events, conferences, and interiors to product shots, food, and portraits. Her work includes a myriad of publications and websites, PR companies, non-profits, and major corporations such as Absolut, Puma, Pepsi, and Adidas.

Leigh Smyth
photographer
itakeyourphotos.net

Starting out in Baltimore, Leigh Smyth has established herself as a multifaceted photographer in Boston. Life behind the lens has transported her from intricate architectural backdrops to exposing personalities at their most intimate.

Renee Trichilo
photographer
reneetrichilo.com

Renee Trichilo loves to take photographs that draw the audience into a captured moment. Her wedding and event photography is fun, classic, journalistic, emotional, and ethereal; in a portrait, she captures the essence.

Additional photography by Savas Studios, Janel Robertson, and Nina Gallant Photography.

Thank you to our interns: Aubry Bracco, Ashley Breckel, Karina Briski, Sarah Clise, Madeline Conner, Shirin Dhuper, Becky Fadden, Amanda Luther, Jennifer Ly, Melisa Miller, Suzanne Nolan, Gina Puccia, and Shauna Toohey.

A Guide to Our Index

Abode — Furniture, home improvement, and interior design
Adorn — Jewelry
Children's — Baby-, children-, and mom-related
Connect — Networking, media, technology, travel, and event services
Details — Gifts, books, small home accessories, florists, and stationery
Enhance — Spas, salons, beauty, and fitness
Pets — Pet-related
Sip Savor — Food and drink
Style — Clothing, shoes, eyewear, handbags, and stylists

Manifest by category

Manifest by category (continued)

Manifest by category (continued)

Manifest Intelligentsia Directory by category

Manifest by neighborhood

Manifest by neighborhood (continued)

Manifest by neighborhood (continued)

CRAVE company™

The CRAVE company innovatively connects small business owners with the customers they crave. We bring together small business communities and fuel them with entrepreneurial know-how and fresh ideas—from business consulting to shopping fairs to new media. The CRAVE company knows what it takes to thrive in the modern marketplace.

CRAVE party®

What Do You Crave?
CRAVEparty is an exclusive, festive, glam-gal gathering of fun, entertainment, personal pampering, specialty shopping, sippin' and noshin', and just hanging with the girls.

CRAVE guides™

Style and Substance. Delivered.
CRAVEguides are the go-to resource for urban-minded women. We celebrate stylish entrepreneurs by showcasing the gutsiest, most creative and interesting proprietors from cities all over the world.

CRAVE business™

A Fresh Approach to Modern Business.
CRAVEbusiness is a social resource network for stylish innovators who own their own business or dream of starting one. Through one-on-one consulting, workshops, and red-carpet access to sage and savvy experts, entrepreneurs meet with others in their fields to get a fresh approach to their business.

Craving Savings

Get the savings you crave with the following participating entreprenesses—one time only!

5 percent off
- [ ] Women on the Move LLC

10 percent off
- [ ] 1-Stop Design Shop, Inc.
- [ ] Ali Magazine
- [ ] The Aries Group
- [ ] Athalia Originals
- [ ] BASIQUES
- [ ] Bow Street Flowers
- [ ] Core de Vie
- [ ] Coven
- [ ] Davis Squared
- [ ] Flock
- [ ] Forty Winks
- [ ] FRENCH + ITALIAN
- [ ] French Dressing
- [ ] Habit
- [ ] Haley's Wines & Spirits
- [ ] Hands of Time
- [ ] Jace Interiors
- [ ] Jessica Sutton Graphic Design
- [ ] JOOS LLC
- [ ] Ken Rothwell's Custom Catering
- [ ] Ken's Kickin Chicken
- [ ] Lantern Financial, LLC
- [ ] Laura Lanes Skin Care
- [ ] Leise Jones Photography
- [ ] Matsu
- [ ] MelOPhoto
- [ ] Modern Pilates
- [ ] Moxie
- [ ] NOMAD
- [ ] Olivia Browning

10 percent off (continued)
- [ ] Orange Nail Studio
- [ ] Penny Schuler Brand Imaging
- [ ] Pinkergreen
- [ ] R&L Associates, Inc.
- [ ] Rhoost
- [ ] Sarra
- [ ] Seed Stitch Fine Yarn
- [ ] Turtle
- [ ] Twinkle Star Baby
- [ ] Two girls shop
- [ ] Urban Elements
- [ ] The Velvet Fly
- [ ] Vianne chocolat
- [ ] The Wine Bottega

15 percent off
- [ ] Ame & Lulu
- [ ] Crush Boutique
- [ ] Fiddlehead
- [ ] Jean therapy
- [ ] LaurieMandato.com
- [ ] Marmalade
- [ ] MOD Boston
- [ ] Modern Millie Vintage & Consignment Shop
- [ ] Mulberry Road
- [ ] Oh Snap!
- [ ] Passport
- [ ] Polka Dog Bakery
- [ ] She
- [ ] Topaz
- [ ] The Urban Hound Hotel
- [ ] Viola Lovely

Craving Savings

20 percent off

- ☐ B'aires
- ☐ BEADworkshop
- ☐ Blush Hair Salon
- ☐ Boston Skin Solutions
- ☐ Cibeline Boston
- ☐ The flat of the hill
- ☐ Geri Costanza MassageWorks, Inc.
- ☐ Grace Sales Co.
- ☐ Harvard Sweet Boutique
- ☐ Helena's
- ☐ In-jean-ius
- ☐ J. Mode
- ☐ Kickass Cupcakes
- ☐ Lola's Urban Vintage
- ☐ Mint Julep
- ☐ Plank
- ☐ Renee Trichilo Photography
- ☐ Savas Studios
- ☐ Scribe Paper & Gift
- ☐ Trust in Tricia
- ☐ Twilight
- ☐ Wish

25 percent off

- ☐ ABClarke Coaching
- ☐ Polished Wardrobe Advising

Use code CRAVE for online discount